C000184034

The Complete Leader

THE NEWWORLD™ BOOK SERIES

The Complete Leader

HOW TO LEAD TO RESULTS

•

Your insight into how to influence change through no-holds-barred leadership based on the fact that **leaders are made and not <u>just</u> born.**

•

Eddie Obeng
Christophe Gillet

pl@pentaclethevbs.com

Copyright Eddie Obeng and Christophe Gillet 2008

The right of Eddie Obeng and Christophe to be identified as the authors of this work has been asserted in accordance with the Copyright, Design and Patents Act 1988

Printed on recycled paper

First published 2008 by PentacleWorks The Virtual Media Company in association with **London Business Press**
PentacleWorks The Virtual Media Company
20 London End
Beaconsfield
Bucks HP9 2JH

All rights reserved. Except for the quotation of short passages for the purposes of criticism and review, no part of this publication may be reproduced, stored in a retrieval system, or transmitted in any form or by any means electronic, mechanical, photocopying, recording or otherwise, without the prior permission of the publisher

A CIP catalogue record for this book is available from the British Library

ISBN 0953486974

Printed and bound by Lulu.com

for Susan & Béatrice

Pentacle has developed a pragmatic "HOW TO" on leadership which cuts through the endless business school case studies and esoteric psychobabble.

Through over 40 years of hands-on leadership experience (the total of the authors' management careers) and decades of teaching, client assignments and research, the authors have established *how leadership actually works* and from that figured out what <u>you</u> need to <u>do</u> and <u>think</u> differently to make you more effective as a 21st century leader.

In the realm of business and organisation management Pentacle has re-written the rules on what is learnt and how it is delivered. Every decent consultancy and management school now uses virtual and e-learning alongside its traditional offer - an approach pioneered since 1994 by Pentacle. Each of our new rules for the new world has spawned an 'industry of activity' and books - from *Say AND not OR* in 1995 (The Tyranny of the or) to *Stakeholders Rule OK* in 1991 (Emotional Intelligence) to *All Constraints to Meatspace* (Virtual Teaming/ Virtual Working/ Virtual Meeting)

Increasingly the OldWorld, linear, Cartesian logic-based approach is being replaced by a balanced human and complexity-based set of concepts and curricula. Although not completely joined up - and in many cases with a nostalgia for the old ideas and an unwillingness to let go of them completely - the business-sphere is moving Pentacle's way

Eddie Obeng and Christophe Gillet's *'The Complete Leader'* is a companion book to *'New Rules for the New World'*.

PENTACLE Learning To Transform:

UNITED KINGDOM	20 London End, Beaconsfield, Buckinghamshire HP9 2JH
FRANCE	Pentacle 45, Avenue Jean-Jaures 69007 LYON
SOUTH AFRICA	Pentacle House 1 Martingale Avenue Hout Bay Cape Town 7806
UNITED STATES	Pentacle Centre of Creativity, Buffalo New York 14092
THE NETHERLANDS	Pentacle House Wassenaar
Telephone Global 24hr:	+44 (0) 1494 678 555
E-mail:	tcl@PentacleTheVBS.com
Website:	http://PentacleTheVBS.com

Contents

To browse by concept, see the list at the end of this book on page 131

ABOUT THE AUTHORS

Eddie Obeng

Eddie is Learning Director of Pentacle The Virtual Business School (Founded 1994). He was previously an Executive Director at Ashridge Management College, having begun his career with Shell.

An agent provocateur **Financial Times**
Our resident guru **Project Manager Today**
Unusual as an academic to back his ideas with his own money **The Sunday Times**
A 'leading revolutionary' **Financial Times**
Eddie's New World analysis was a vital catalyst in our programme of change and reinvention in Sony. Plus his unique style added greatly to making it highly entertaining along the way **Miles Flint Sony**
High energy, inspiring, thought provoking and highly effective **Judy Gibbons Microsoft**.

Unlike most management gurus, though, he is not a great one for strategy. Indeed, he says 'strategic' is sometimes used as another word for 'loss-making'. Instead, he concentrates on getting to the basics of what makes businesses work - and it is this realism and grounded-ness that has brought clients as varied as supermarket group Tesco, kitchen and bathroom company Magnet, and electronics company Sony to his Pentacle Virtual Business School.

Christophe Gillet

Christophe is Director of Europe for Pentacle The Virtual Business School one of the world's most innovative learning businesses. In a previous life, he was Director of Business Innovation for SONY Business Europe. He spent most of his career in sales and marketing, leading multinational & multicultural business teams.

Christophe has 15 years of experience in High-Tech Business-to-Business operations. He has first hand experience in leadership of change and innovation, including new business creation, business modeling, innovative project management, value marketing... He has been responsible for successfully re-engineering profit centres from 'product/technology' to 'customer/value' driven.

Christophe has practical leadership experience in multi cultural environments of transformational change management, including creating Virtual teams to deliver more value. He brings all this experience to his work at Pentacle.

How this book came about[1]

When I was a kid, I never dreamt of being 'a leader'. Nor did my parents, I bet. Leaders at that time were people like Gandhi, Martin Luther King or Captain Kirk. In companies and institutions people worked hard and "kept their noses clean", climbing step by step the slippery ladder of hierarchy with the aim of becoming, one day, a 'manager', a knowledgeable, trustworthy & responsible person who 'kept the ship on an even keel'. Today, companies are <u>full</u> of 'managers' (even my plumber now wants to be called a 'water streams manager') but it seems that something in the world has changed which makes them uncomfortable and unfulfilled in their role, something which forces them to change their approach, behaviour and skills. They now secretly dream of becoming corporate Hindis.

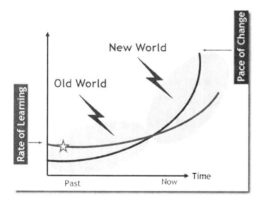

Welcome to the NewWorld! These days we live now in a <u>business world which changes faster than our capability to learn.</u> This NewWorld^{TM} forces us to cope with more and more complex

---

[1] This section is fiction and only here to avoid disappointment for the readers who bought this book hoping to learn more from Franck

situations, whilst leaving us with less and less opportunity to 'predict' or even 'imagine' our future.

In such complex and uncertain situations, people do not feel engaged, emotion often overcomes logic, traditional planning doesn't work, standard budgeting processes are made obsolete, risk management becomes a main factor of success, rigid strategies do not make sense, leadership styles must be interchangeable, teams need to be seen as virtual entities, etc …

More importantly for managers, "doing what we've always done" no longer implies "getting what we've always got". Simply operating efficiently no longer guarantees success. Everything in the organisation needs to reviewed and re-invented to make it operate effectively. Everything, including: hierarchy, management, decision making, teamwork, expertise, communication. The list is endless.

Do you remember the good old days? (A few million years ago actually) when all of us were fish of some sort? (The lawyers of today were sharks then!) We spent our time developing embryonic legs and thinking hard about how to get out of the water in order to become, one day, what we now call 'a human being' Would the skills of swimming still be useful once we had to move over the ground? Today, the challenge managers face seems to be analogous. They are trying to leave a well know world, a Cartesian, more linear, more local, more face to face world for one which is global-sized, fast changing, chaotic and largely in cyberspace. The OldWorld has its own own set of rules and best practices, which managers know and understand,

However, on entering the NewWorld their past experience is of limited use and even dangerous sometimes.

Unfortunately, most managers have not come across 'my' secret treasure map.

In a world...	In a world ...
... of low complexity	... of high complexity
... which changes slowly	... which changes quickly & permanently
... where learning has a long shelf-life	... where learning has a short shelf-life,
... where (some) individuals 'know' and where the eldest is the most knowledgeable	... where no-one can pretend to 'know' and where all provide a part of the knowledge
... where doing more of the same is the focus	... where differentiation is the main focus
YOU MANAGE	**YOU LEAD**
... you are part of a top-down decision flow because of your hierarchical position	... you are part of a sphere of influence in which seniority as little to do with influence
... you contribute through experience & expertise	... you contribute by influence & negotiation
... you are part of an "expert group" (department, division, etc ...)	... you cannot succeed without other groups
... you have a hierarchical role in that group	... you are part of a larger 'virtual team' over which you have no hierarchical control
... you have your own management style developed over the years to fit the purpose	... you develop several leadership styles in order to adapt to different and unstable situations
... your role is to manage (and improve) today	... your role is to manage today AND build tomorrow
... your role is to avoid risks	... your role is to balance risks vs opportunities
... you have clear and stable 'mission & objectives' that you understand and cascade down	... you have a 'strategy' which helps you understand your role in the big picture
... you are part of a value chain	... you are part of a money making network
... you manage processes	... you lead projects
... you have a Boss	... you have Stakeholders
...	...

Good old Franck[2]! My favourite challenging partner. Always something new and provocative to unveil! Always on the cutting edge! He handed me this map with a mischievous smile and said, "I drew this map on my expedition to find the *New Rules for the New World*. If you can crack the code you'll be able to decipher the map and discover where the treasure is. If you do that you can be sure there's a good chance Pentacle will become the global thought leader in leadership development ...." And that's how this book started ...

---

[2] Franck is the enigmatic guru who leads the voyage of discovery in New Rules for the New World E Obeng Wiley Publishing ISBN 3854362498
[5] Making Re-engineering Happen E Obeng FT Publishing ISBN 027362220X

The Complete Leader

HOW TO LEAD TO RESULTS

WHY LEADERSHIP?

Are you officially the most powerful or senior person in your organisation? I suspect not. So what right do you have to pick up a book on leadership? Surely leadership comes from 'the top' and if that's not you then you need to put this book down now!

No! Of course not. The reason you've picked up this book is because the past ten years have revolutionalised what real leadership is in our complex and fast changing NewWorld^{TM}.

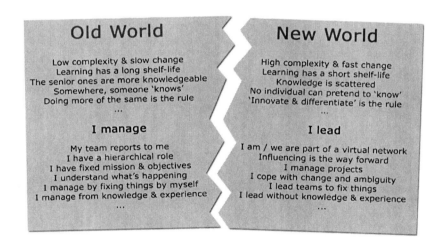

Old World

Low complexity & slow change
Learning has a long shelf-life
The senior ones are more knowledgeable
Somewhere, someone 'knows'
Doing more of the same is the rule
...

I manage

My team reports to me
I have a hierarchical role
I have fixed mission & objectives
I understand what's happening
I manage by fixing things by myself
I manage from knowledge & experience
...

New World

High complexity & fast change
Learning has a short shelf-life
Knowledge is scattered
No individual can pretend to 'know'
'Innovate & differentiate' is the rule
...

I lead

I am / we are part of a virtual network
Influencing is the way forward
I manage projects
I cope with change and ambiguity
I lead teams to fix things
I lead without knowledge & experience
...

And that is why you are trying to get your head around leadership, what it means for you, how leadership could help you in your career and make your life happier. That is why you are interested in how you can be more effective at it. Well you've come to the right place. Making you more effective at leadership is what this book aims to do in clear, straight-forward language and explanations. The topic of leadership is complex but not complicated, so stick with us and you'll come out brilliantly.

CHAPTER 1 LEADING TO RESULTS

In which we begin to explain the 'problem' of leadership

The Leader

> I wanna be the leader
>
> I wanna be the leader
>
> Can I be the leader?
>
> Can I? I can?
>
> Promise? Promise?
>
> Yippee, I'm the leader
>
> I'm the leader
>
> OK what shall we do?

Roger McGough

You're on a training course - An experiential training course. One of those courses where the tutor sets up an exercise, something like one of those ranking exercises - you're lost in the desert - stuck in the Arctic - crashed on the moon. You and eleven other colleagues have to put in correct order 20 random objects. You have 30 minutes.

A week later - it feels like a week but it's only 45 minutes later - you are suffering the acute embarrassment of watching yourselves on the play back of the video. It's a shambles and there is real evidence, so denial isn't an option. What went wrong?

Now the tutor is waffling on and on. Some stuff about leadership and how, by not being clear on your roles and accountabilities and by not having a leader to help to define the goal, you have gone off track.

One of your group comments that you are all colleagues and so it would not feel right to have someone bossing the rest of you about.

The tutor is trying to explain some semantic difference between a boss or manager and a leader but you are lost in your own thoughts. You are thinking leadership is bunk. At work, in the real world, the manager simply manages. The reporting lines lead to very senior people who take all the decisions and make sure that everyone does what they are supposed to, period.

Anyway, only last month your organisation's best project manager was fired for doing this "leadership stuff" instead of just delivering! For the past three years he'd been responsible for a series of expansion projects, opening a series of new offices and branches across Europe. Nine months ago he was given a smallish project on 'web2.0-enabling' the entire organisation. This was seen as their 'opportunity to demonstrate leadership qualities'. Nine months later six key staff had quit complaining of 'bullying', a 'lack of empowerment' and a 'lack of opportunity to creatively explore the issues.' On top of that the consultants who put the detailed implementation plan together had left the company £250k richer. The project manager had left empty handed shortly afterwards.

No, you're not convinced. Anyway, you've read somewhere that leaders are born that way. So you are either a leader or you're not. Fortunately the tutor has stopped talking and it's time for a coffee break.

CHAPTER 2 **WHY DO WE NEED LEADERS?**

_____

In which we explain why and how
the 'shortage of leaders(hip)' has arisen.

In my country we go to prison first,
and then become president.
Nelson Mandela

Leaders! Who needs them?

Well, actually, we do if we are carrying out any activity
which requires an input from more than ourselves and
which is 'new' to others.

Traditionally, **the purpose of an organisation was to
organise.** In the industrial age this equated closely with the
division of labour. So by 'organise' we meant: to take a
large complex but recurring job and divide it amongst a
larger group of people. This idea is centuries old, the most
famous example being Adam Smith's organisation of the
pin factory where, by dividing the steps of making a pin
into eighteen distinct operations among specialised men,
each of whom did a repetitive job, the productivity of the
factory was increased by 24,000 percent! The intention
was efficiency, business-as-usual meant repetition.   So
does that mean there was no 'change' occurring? No, there
was certainly change occurring but the change was in the
metal of the pin - not in the tasks people carried out. The
people did the same actions day-in day-out. This is an

important point.   Change happened routinely in the processes but not in the systems, structures or people[5].

The traditional adage was 'Give people clarity in their jobs'. A job was a repeated activity which was owned by the individual.   As long as the structure was in place to allow the jobs to fit together to deliver the overall results, all was well. **In the Old World[6] most organisations could learn and adapt faster than the world was changing,** so the structure and interrelationships between jobs could be clarified and controlled.

Change in the organisation or in the industry tended to be an unusual and discrete set of events.   Most of **business activity was focused on maintaining and delivering more-of-the-same.**   The net result was that we built organisations which were compartmentalised into simple hierarchical structures with the most experienced people at the top, controlling the actions of all those below through a linear command and control system.   When structural or systemic change was required it needed a significant amount of effort, feasibility research and advice taken until it was clear to the people at "the top", the ones with the power, <u>What</u> was to be achieved (Outcome) and <u>How</u> it was to be done (Method/ Technology).

Once this point of clarity was reached these people were now well placed to provide **leadership** and all those below knew this and would duly comply.

---

[5] Making Re-engineering Happen E Obeng FT Publishing ISBN 027362220X
[6] New Rules for the New World E Obeng Wiley Publishing ISBN 3854362498

If the change was particularly significant a 'special project' of some sort would be set up to focus the efforts on the resources and control them.

This approach is still used in several situations today. For example, it is common for consultants to deploy this structure for post merger integration activities.

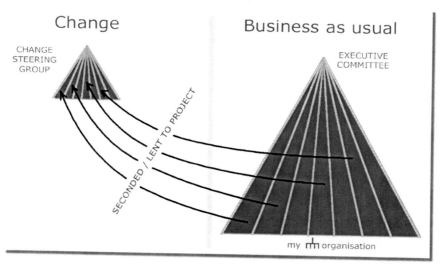

Unfortunately for all the people who still adhere to these centuries-old concepts, the world has changed significantly. **Today the pace of change in our business or organisational environment regularly outstrips our ability to learn and change.** By now you will have people who "report" to you whose jobs you are unsure of, carrying out activities <u>you</u> have never done in <u>your</u> career and don't fully understand. You will have discovered that **your plans and budgets are often obsolete before the ink is dry.** You will have found that the youngest staff member, just recruited into your team can potentially bring more value to the customer or more money to the organisation than the rest of the team put together. And you will have found **that a significant amount of your activity involves people from outside your direct area of the hierarchy,** with them trying to involve or influence you or you doing the same to them. In addition, the organisation is complex and geographically spread. **You've probably also understood the real challenge of globalisation.** It is not what most commentators think. After all, Marco Polo began trading with China 700 years ago and 3000 years ago the Egyptians traded actively with the Middle East. Remember the Dutch black Ships? The Triangular Trade between Africa, America and Europe? The issue is not commerce. Do the people at the top still have the ability to impose their will on all the people affected by the changes they propose? No. Such direct power is severely reduced. People can appear to be complying whilst actually resisting the change. Many of the **changes introduced are unfamiliar and cause people to react emotionally** rather than entirely logically. **The real issue is how to lead organisations which operate across the globe, from multiple cultures from within another culture - yours.** The issue in short is that "there are many stakeholders[7] throughout the organisation all of whom need to be aligned if the changes are to deliver the benefits sought. Stakeholders who help the effort of the change and those who have to live with its results must alter their own personal behaviour and actions in order that the benefits can be reaped.

---

[7] Stakeholders is the term we use to describe people who have an influence over the success of any change. In our new world stakeholders are often not directly involved, are often almost invisible until it's too late and often exist outside your part of the organisation or even the organisation itself.

Not only are the changes to be introduced unfamiliar but they exist within a cacophony of other noise. That noise is data. In a world where a single newspaper contains more data than a person in the 17th century would have received in their entire lifetime; In the Old World all we needed was a little data to keep us on track with the occasional big bang of revolution. But now the big bang is constant 'sound and fury' and our still, small voice has still got to be heard for people to be aligned.

Finally, there are far more changes required than before and it is unlikely that there will be enough 'most senior' people to manage them. This means that most change 'agents' or managers will have to move, emotionally engage and influence people who can be senior to them or even in other functions, departments or businesses, or in different locations around the planet or living and working in a completely different 'cultural bubble', in short: stakeholders. <u>They cannot be 'managed'</u>.

This NewWorld works to different rules especially when it comes to change.

This is when complete leadership starts to be relevant. Because **you can only *manage* people you have authority over, but you can (and need to) *lead* anyone**.

Think of a good movie you have been to watch lately. The director isn't your boss but somehow they make you behave a certain way - sit in the cinema for almost two hours following the twists and turns of their plot. (In a bad film you walk out, day dream etc.)

So what is the difference between management and leadership? Is there one?

How did you become a manager? I guess for most people, they hang about in the organization for a while. Eventually another manager approaches them, taps them on the top of the head and says "Thou art now a Manager. Arise and take thy car keys." And they become a manager.

In other words, **other managers** make **you** a manager.

How do you become a leader? Do other leaders make you one? Do you decide that you are one and then you become one?

Two short scenarios:

One of your colleagues turns up for work wearing a bright blue and orange suit with shoes to match. The next week a dozen more of your colleagues turn up for work dressed exactly the same way.

One of your colleagues turns up for work wearing a bright blue and orange suit and spends all day telling everyone that this is the height of fashion. Everyone laughs and no one is ever seen wearing anything even remotely as ridiculous.

Strange but true, but it is the action of **other people (followers)** deciding to follow you that **makes you a leader**

CHAPTER 3   WHY DO FOLLOWERS FOLLOW?

In which we explain
the connection between followers and leaders

For every action there is an equal and opposite reaction

Isaac Newton

For every action there is an equal and opposite criticism

Anon

 **But what exactly makes people follow?** In the OldWorld people (and that includes your children) would follow you because of your position in the organisation, status, birthright, or simply because you were the only game in town. The NewWorld has made this more complex. In many organisations employees are "empowered" which means that they get a say in who they decide to follow.

Have you ever followed anyone? You're probably shaking your head so let me rephrase the question:

You're into sport, art, whatever! And there is someone much 'better' in your eyes than you. Do you remember copying their style? Begging them to show you how they did it? Eating and maybe even dressing like them - hoping some of their genius would rub off on you?

You really wanted to learn what they knew. **Learning** can be a strong driver for followers.

Or perhaps this one:

You just couldn't put the book down. The way they described the future was stunning, you wanted to learn more about what the future could look like and even more importantly you wanted to be part of that future. You wanted to help to make it happen.

The compelling **Vision** was driving you to follow.

Do you remember when you were younger and more naïve, wanting to be part of something?

All your friends were sporting strange haircuts and you had one too or perhaps it was a type of bicycle or a particular games console? Either way you nagged your parents, or secretly snuck off and had the haircut. Do you remember the passion you had, the yearning to be 'one of the gang? You decided to join in, to follow because you wanted to be included.

Inclusion is a very strong driver for followers.

And here's another one:

You're out for the evening with friends - on a skiing holiday with your family - either way it's a complete shambles. No one will say what they want to do and no one is really sure what to do, how long it will take or even how to start it. It's getting tense and boring and then someone lays out the whole plan of what should and will be done to maximise the pleasure available in the time. Not only that but they highlight each person's contribution to making things better. You are just so delighted to have some direction you'll go along with anything they suggest. Anything to stop this drifting.

Providing **direction** can really help people to decide to follow.

Or finally, this one:

You'd never heard music so exciting or a singer, speaker, presenter so electrifyingly energetic. They seemed to be having an intensely good time and it was so palpable you could feel it. You wanted to jump up and shout dance, whatever. You were motivated.

Motivation is a reason to follow.

What we've done is to establish why on earth anyone would want to follow. To find out the 'What's in it for me?' and then we've grouped the different 'triggers under these five groups which seem to cover everything. We could have used a different grouping but these five seem to work very well.

Understanding why and individual would follow you is a step away from understanding why a group, a country or even the whole world would follow you.

Followers must have a (rational or emotional) reason to follow

CHAPTER 4 HOW DOES LEADERSHIP ACTUALLY WORK?

In which we strip leadership bare
and explain the 'mechanics'

*For every ineffective manager there is
an equal and opposite leader!*

Gillet

Yesterday I was listening to a radio quiz comedy show. The topic was a 'farewell' trip that the country's Prime Minister was making just before leaving office. The show referred to the Prime Minister as 'our leader' which made me confused about the comments that followed. One of the questions was if the Prime Minister wanted to depart to the sound of applause and clapping where should he go? The answers included, 'Under a very large stone,' 'Somewhere very far abroad, probably one of the habitats that global warming would obliterate,' 'Nowhere in this country' and many others. I got the distinct impression that the comments were not being made by followers of this leader. I also noticed that the studio audience laughed loudly and burst into applause at some of the more caustic comments. Somehow this senior politician, although still the 'chief executive', was no longer a leader.

 There is a game I play with groups after lunch on some of the courses I teach. It's called TouchTips.   Yes,   I   know, unfortunate   name   and   I   always   get   the   8-year-old's question. I secretly brief half the group and explain that we will be playing in silence and for two rounds. The first is **The Push Round.** In this round they are to select a safe place in the room and gently try to manoeuvre (by pushing) their partner towards it. In the second round, **The Pull Round,** the goal is the same only this time they back away from their partner. I ask that after each round they must clap and applaud enthusiastically. I then pair them up with the other half of the course, the unsuspecting soon-to-be-victims. I explain the rules of the game that hands must be held up in front of each person with the fingertips of each pair touching (hence the title). The most important rule is that the fingertips must never part. I tell them a winning team will be selected and suggest we play TouchTips to win! The briefed partner starts to push towards the goal. **Their push is met by an equal resistance** and all that happens is you end up with the pair pushing energetically against each other and making almost no progress or movement. We applaud and cheer leaving the un-briefed half of the group bewildered. Then I announce "Round Two" and remind them of the rule that **finger tips must not come apart.** The backward movement often takes the un-briefed partner by surprise.   By now they are conditioned to resist and have geared up to push <u>really</u> hard. The movement follows **and there is a fluid dance as the un-briefed group is 'pulled' along.** Occasionally one

of the briefed team ends up with their back to the wall - pinned to it by an enthusiastic partner! Again applause.

Then the debrief. Questions are directed to the un-briefed half. What was that about? How did you feel about the silence when you asked for an explanation and didn't get any communication? Why did you push back? How much movement was there? Which were the only pairs where there was movement - Was it always when the pusher was larger or the partner had delicate fingers or fingernails? What did Round One versus Round Two illustrate? So if you can only manage people you are stronger than, what about leadership and so on. By the end of the debrief the difference between leadership and management is absolutely clear. **Management is about using the formal power and authority you have over others to get things done** ('Push'). But you can only manage people you have more power and authority than. Leadership is something else. It relies on the fingers remaining 'glued' to each other. That is, the follower's willingness to follow and the leader's willingness to lead! ('Pull')

The final question of the debrief - which is always asked but never followed through for an answer is **"What do you do in real life, as a leader, to ensure your fingertips and the fingertips of your followers keep touching?"**

So we know why leaders(hip) is needed and what the potential followers are looking for. But surely that's of little practical use. Everyone knows that leaders are born, they are people with charisma, often over six feet tall. Since there are only (not?) so many people who are 6 foot 6 and charismatic you are bound to have a shortage of them.

Do you fit this description? If not I'm sorry but there is no hope for you!

In my lifetime I've read many shelf loads of books on leadership. First when I was an aspiring manager trying to further my career, then as an MBA student and finally as someone trying to teach the subject. I've also been on corridors of courses. At the end of every course I've always been left with a sort of magical-mystical view of leadership. After discussing political leaders, watching Apollo 13 and the like you were left with the impression that actually in-spite of all you had been told and all the psychometric tests, there was actually either an innate thing these leaders had (because they often couldn't explain their own success in their autobiographies) or there was some secret they kept on pain of death!

This intrigued me and propelled my curiosity. And then I discovered that the 'secret' was not so secret. I'll use an analogy to explain it.

Imagine yourself on the beach on a beautiful day, reclining in your deck chair. You decide to listen to some music. You're in the mood for some randomness in your life so instead of reaching for your trusty mp3 player you decide to listen to the radio. You get your old analogue non-digital radio out of your bag and turn it on. You 'tune' it in and music gushes forth. You nod your head to the beat and tap your fingers appreciatively.

You receive 'cool' engaging music which you really enjoy.

Followers have their receivers switched on to listen out for the cool engaging leadership vibes.

Followers
'Receive'

They are keen to LEARN

They share your VISION

They feel INCLUSION

They receive DIRECTION

They get MOTIVATION

The transmitter has to transmit in order for the receivers to receive. In the radio example they transmit radio waves but you receive music which is what you are interested in (most of us are not in interested in radio waves per se). The transmitter has the responsibility of making sure that their message is transformed into radio waves and beamed hard and far enough for you to receive them. And to make sure you have information on how to find them or tune in. The same applies to leaders. Leaders don't *'transmit'* 'inclusion' or 'learning'. How could they possibly do this? They transmit something which you can interpret locally as inclusion or learning. What they actually transmit is the **behaviour** you see them exhibit, the **emotions** they surround themselves with, the priority of **actions** they pursue and the way they seem to **think** through the challenges they face.

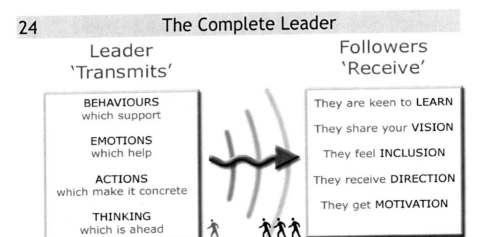

This model of transmit and receive is at the heart of COMPLETE LEADERSHIP.

This is Leadership stripped to its bare essentials without all the fluff and flannel that academics and consultants love to add.

This is Leadership stripped to it's bare essentials but which leaves nothing crucial out! Leadership which looks at the challenge not only from the leader's point of view but also from that of the followers

And that is how leadership actually works. Now it's no longer a secret and if you were born with it, great for you, but you've lost your advantage because we can all do it now!

CHAPTER 5 WHY DOESN'T TRANSMIT-RECEIVE ALWAYS WORK PERFECTLY?

In which we explain the conditional nature of Transmit-Receive

A man doesn't have himself killed for a half-pence a day or for a petty distinction. You must speak to the soul in order to electrify him.

Napoleon

I left you on the beach enjoying the music from the weather and the great sunshine.

Unfortunately the weather has changed suddenly and the rain is tipping down. Periodically illuminated by sheet lightning. You rush indoors for cover and settle back into listening to your music but notice a high level of distortion and background noise. The problem you face is that your medium has changed. For signals of less than 10 GHz raindrops will affect transmission. In addition the lightning is adding a bit of noise of its own. And this is one of the key filters to the transmitted message reaching the receiver without distortion.

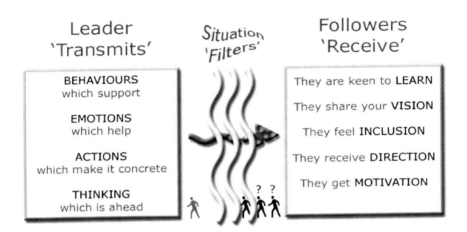

Leader 'Transmits'

BEHAVIOURS
which support

EMOTIONS
which help

ACTIONS
which make it concrete

THINKING
which is ahead

Situation 'Filters'

Followers 'Receive'

They are keen to LEARN

They share your VISION

They feel INCLUSION

They receive DIRECTION

They get MOTIVATION

In organisational change, the concept of 'medium' translates to the situation (or more accurately what I describe as the **'type of change'**). In our NewWorld, where pace of change often outstrips speed of learning, change can make us feel many different emotions. Sometimes we feel confident, at other times excited and challenged, at other times comfortable in our abilities but unsure of the value and at other times frightened, embarrassed, confused and concerned.

These feelings correlate very well with the type of change we are trying to lead. Feeling confident often equates with change we recognise and have the capability to deal with. The goals are clear and the methods are known. It's so straightforward, even if not simple, you could almost equate it to **'painting-by-numbers'**. Feeling excited and challenged are emotions which often accompany a change for which a clear goal is available - often a very attractive goal. However the methods and means are missing and that's why we experience the combination of excitement and challenge. Feeling comfortable and yet unsure and questioning happens when the change requires from us our capabilities but without clarity on what will be gained or achieved. It's not that we don't know how to carry out the activities required it's just we're unsure of what the outcome will be. The final set of emotions correlates very well with change where both the goals and the means and methods are uncertain. **These 'types of change' produce different 'filtering' characteristics and can completely distort the leader's transmission.**

First a little bit of jargon to make it easier to remember the four types of change.

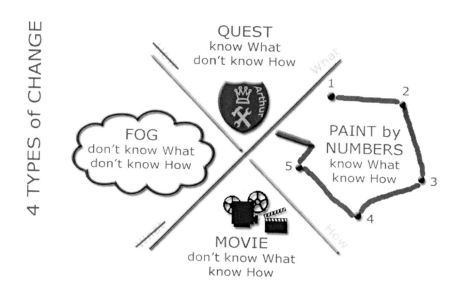

I need you to be patient and wait for Chapter 8 to fully explore the effect of the distortion. At this stage I only want to explain the distortion of the situation.

There's another reason why the potential followers might not receive your message. Could it be that they have actually tuned to a different frequency? We all know how, before you purchase the car, trainers or sunglasses you really fancy, they appear rare and not very common. However, the moment you drive the car out of the showroom or put on the trainers or sunglasses, the roads seem traffic-jammed with exactly the same model and everyone seems to be wearing the same brand!

The problem quite simply is that **a person's mind-set actually influences the messages they receive.** You actively notice issues and items in the foreground but ignore the 'noise' in the background. Your mind-set is the list of things in the foreground for you. In terms of mind-set, things happening in the background might not be happening at all.

I remember the first time I read Claes Janssen's[8] analysis of psychological readiness for change which was heavy going but had at its centre a model of a four roomed apartment. It set me thinking about 'rooms in your head' that your mind could occupy. And a cartoon series I loved as a kid, called the Numskulls which involved little people who lived in your head and depending on what they were up to you felt the effects. For example, if they left the tap on by accident your nose would drip, hammering nails into the wall to put up a new picture was a headache, sweeping dust would make you sneeze and so on. I have imagined a set of rooms in a person's head.

I think about the rooms as the various places a **mind-set** could 'hang out'.

You can tell which room their 'mind-set' is in simply by listening to what they say and watching how they behave. Go on, have a go, try to guess a typical sentence from someone who is in the attic of arrogance. How does that compare to someone in the analysis-paralysis pit? Exactly!

---

[8] The Four Rooms of Change *Förändringens fyra rum* C Janssen Wahlström & Widstrand, 1996

The problem you have as a leader is that the mind-set acts as a filter, screening out the messages you're transmitting unless they match with the follower's mind-set.

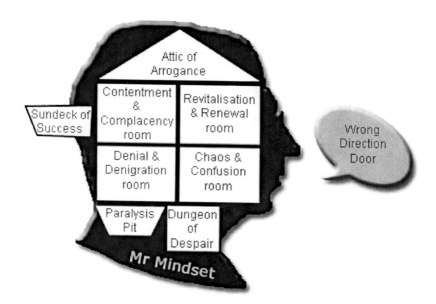

What do you think happens if you start to explain how the change is to happen to a person whose mind-set is out 'bathing in the glory of past success'? What do you think happens when you use a logical explanation on someone whose mind-set is lost in the 'dungeon of despair'? I think you'll have got the point.

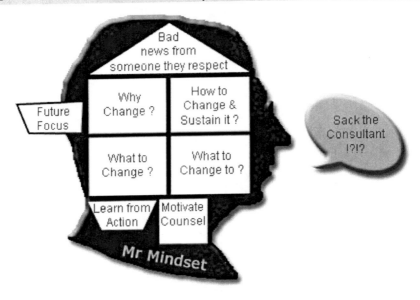

To be effective, a leader must often tell the "whole story from Why to How" as a way of herding the followers together. This makes getting followers easier and more effective later.

CHAPTER 6 LEADERSHIP: TERMS AND CONDITIONS

In which you agree to our terms and conditions or stop reading NOW!

I wish to be cremated. One tenth of my ashes shall be given to my agent as written in our contract.

Groucho Marx

If you google "The World's Worst Leader" what is intriguing is not that you get a list of people who tried to lead but had no followers but that you get a list of people whose followers have allowed them political or totalitarian power. **The reason they are described as the <u>worst</u> because they have "mis-led". They have led to a place where humanity has been impoverished by their leadership. It is not the skills or their process of leadership which is an issue, it is their <u>intent</u>.**

So you might not be Hitler or Pol Pot but you can still do a lot of damage if you have effective leadership skills. For a start you may not know the difference between leading change and leading improvement. Do you? What is the difference between change and improvement? Do you know that you should try to avoid leading change and focus on leading improvement? What's the difference? I want you to imagine that I moved the position of the laptop I'm typing this manuscript on 0.3 centimeters to the left. Has that made the reading experience better for you? Is the learning clearer? **You see, you can "change" anything but improvements are the few things that take you closer to your goals or make life more enjoyable or enriching**. As a leader you MUST understand the difference between the two, between change and improvement.

Another way leaders mis-lead is to start something which makes the future much worse than it would otherwise have been. In this case it may not have been your intent but instead it is your <u>lack of foresight or competence</u>. It's often referred to as the Law of Unintended Consequences. I call it the Law of short-sighted, arrogant, thick leaders. You may have seen many examples. They range from invading a country and not realising that the locals are unlikely to want you to stay, to starting a price war without realising the damage to the industry's reputation in the customers' eyes, to limiting the number of carry on bags through a transit airport without realising that this would upset millions of travellers and cause them to avoid the airport completely!

And that is your challenge and your promise. As you enter the next part of this book you will learn how to become an irresistible Complete Leader, so **I must ask of you a solemn promise that you do NOT *mis*-lead**. If you cannot promise this, you are <u>not</u> allowed to read the rest of the book. All copyright restrictions are applied and reading the rest of the book is illegal!

I the undersigned agree to comply with the aforementioned terms and conditions, to always lead-to-results and never mis-lead.

On completion of this book I will strive to be an exemplary COMPLETE LEADER.

Signed _____

Name (in capitals) _____

Date _____

Witness

Name_____ Signature_____

Address _____

CHAPTER 7 HOW DO I NEED TO CHANGE TO LEAD CHANGE?

In which you begin to reflect on the changes you have to make to yourself to be a Complete Leader

This is the true joy of life: the being used for a purpose recognised by yourself as a mighty one; the being thoroughly worn out before you are thrown on the scrap-heap; the being a force of nature, instead of a feverish, selfish little clod of ailments and grievances, complaining that the world will not devote itself to making you happy.

Bernard Shaw

So how do <u>you</u> need to change to lead change? Well it depends on you, the change you intend to lead and the people you need to get to follow you.

1. **The First Insight is to understand the type of change situation you actually like to lead in.** This often correlates with whether or not you'll actually put yourself forward as a leader and also often with the behaviours, emotions you show, actions you take and thought processes you use as your default. It gives a good indication of your current habits and

now I must offer a disclaimer. Just because you <u>like</u> to lead a particular type of change doesn't mean that you are actually any good at it! The following quiz measures preference <u>not</u> capability

Only dead fish swim with the stream

SquarePeg™ Quiz
(My Preferred Leadership Style)

For each pair of answers please **tick** the **one** that best answers the question for *you*.

1. **When I am responsible for delivering change, I feel more comfortable if I am...**

a	b	c	d	e	f

   a. The most experienced
   b. Challenging others to think and do new things

2. **When I am responsible for delivering change, I feel more comfortable if I am...**

a	b	c	d	e	f

   c. Having to spend time to make sure that I understand how I can use my skills to achieve the objective
   d. Getting on with the work

3. **When I am responsible for delivering change, I feel more comfortable if I am...**

a	b	c	d	e	f

   e. Exploring several alternative routes
   f. Finding out with my team what is expected of us

4. **When I have been asked to deliver change I feel happiest if I am...**

a	b	c	d	e	f

   a. Left with clear objectives and methodology to get on with it
   b. Allowed to change and redefine the needs myself, as I see them

5. **When I have been asked to deliver change I feel happiest if I am...**

a	b	c	d	e	f

   d. Given clear accountabilities and responsibilities
   e. Allowed to find my own routes to deliver the specified deliverables

6. **When I have been asked to deliver change I feel happiest if I am...**

a	b	c	d	e	f

   c. Allowed to comment on the deliverables and suggest alternatives based on our methods
   f. Not constrained to specific detailed deliverables as long as I produce something of value

7. **When I have to manage a project I feel most confident if I can...**

a	b	c	d	e	f

   a. Use experience I have gained from the past
   b. Be given a decent sized budget and access to resources and left to get on

8. When I have to manage a project I feel most confident if I can...

		a	b	c	d	e	f
d.	Choose to work with people who are experienced and professional						
f.	Choose to work with people who I respect who are creative and communicative						

9. When I have to manage a project I feel most confident if I can...

		a	b	c	d	e	f
c.	Choose a wide range of different people to help me work out what I should be doing						
e.	Choose to work with people who are dedicated and single minded						

10. When it's down to me to get others to work on a project, I like to think that I can...

		a	b	c	d	e	f
a.	Provide the right answers to my team and other stakeholders						
b.	Provide the intellectual challenge to others to make them come up with the best answers						

11. When it's down to me to get others to work on a project, I like to think that I can...

		a	b	c	d	e	f
c.	Make sure that people are asking the right questions						
f.	Make sure that people are trying to understand what is happening around them						

12. When it's down to me to get others to work on a project, I like to think that I can...

		a	b	c	d	e	f
d.	Make sure that people are searching for the right answers						
e.	Check the answers people are coming up with						

13. When I have to work with others I see myself as...

		a	b	c	d	e	f
a.	The person who is making sure that we do it better this time than we did last time						
b.	The person who is making sure that we do it differently this time than we did last time						

14. When I have to work with others I see myself as...

		a	b	c	d	e	f
c.	The person who makes sure we apply all our skills and knowledge to the problem at hand						
e.	The person who makes sure that we invent new ways of doing things						

15. When I have to work with others I see myself as...

		a	b	c	d	e	f
d.	The person who can be relied upon to give clear instructions and guidance						
f.	The person who can come up with ways of progressing if we get stuck						

16. I am more likely to say...

		a	b	c	d	e	f
a.	'How are we doing according to the plan?'						
b.	'How about if we try this?'						

17. I am more likely to say...

		a	b	c	d	e	f
d.	'I've been thinking about this for some time.'						
e.	'It would be really great if ...'						

18. I am more likely to say...

		a	b	c	d	e	f
c.	'I think we will do a better job this time.'						
f.	'I think that we are going to have to experiment.'						

19. I am more likely to say...

		a	b	c	d	e	f
a.	'I prefer evolutionary change.'						
b.	'I prefer revolutionary change.'						

20. I am more likely to say...

		a	b	c	d	e	f
c.	'Let's spend some more time working out precisely what we should be aiming at.'						
d.	'J.F.D.I.! (Just Do It!)'						

21. I am more likely to say...

		a	b	c	d	e	f
e.	'At least we now know how not to do it.'						
f.	'One step at a time.'						

22. Others see me as...

		a	b	c	d	e	f
a.	A person who conforms						
b.	A person who is happy to change a plan at a moment's notice						

23. Others see me as...

		a	b	c	d	e	f
d.	Measured systematic and methodical						
e.	Often seduced by a cause						

24. Others see me as...

		a	b	c	d	e	f
e.	Capable in my area of knowledge and skills						
f.	Needing the stimulation of constant change						

WHAT TYPES OF CHANGE DO YOU PREFER TO LEAD?

	Please calculate the number of ticks for each letter answer. (The total should come to 24)	a	b	c	d	e	f
TOTALS							
a.							
b.							
c.							
d.							
e.							
f.							

Transfer scores and do sums!

							Code
	+b	-c		+e		=	P
-a	+b		-d		+f	=	I
+a		+c		-e		=	C
+a	-b		+d		-f	=	A

Code	Score Please circle the largest	Descrip-tion	The types of change preferred are:
P		Pioneer	**Pioneers** feel most comfortable with Going on **Quests**
I		Innovator	**Innovators** feel most comfortable with Walking in the **Fog**
C		Craftsman	**Craftsmen** feel most comfortable with Making a **Movie**
A		Adaptor	**Adaptors** feel most comfortable with **Painting-by-Numbers**
	Negative scores mean you tend to avoid/ shy away from leading this way/ type of change		The score is not a measure of how good you are at this type of leadership only your preference for the role

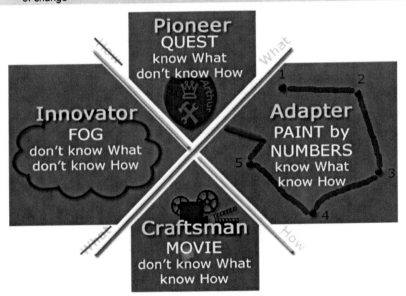

2. The Second Insight you can get of yourself on how you need to change to lead change is related to how you <u>actually spend your time</u> at the moment.

First identify how 'they' (a given individual, group or community) would most likely expect to be led at this particular period of time …

Target Person/Group	What they are seeking in order to follow you				
	Inclusion	Motivation	Direction	Vision	Learning

Now select a recent day you can remember in clear detail and complete the table below:

Time Slot	Your activity: Behaviours demonstrated, Actions carried out, Emotions expressed, Thinking Shared	Target Group	Impact of your activity H-High/ L-Low				
			I	M	D	V	L
0800							
0900							
10:00							
11:00							
12:00							
13:00							
14:00							
15:00							
16:00							
17:00							
18:00							

If, like most of us, you realise that you spent very little time on activities which generate and engage followers (that is building your leadership), you may wish to reverse this process and, using the same table, plan your next week making sure that your activities will match your followers' needs.

3.   The Third Insight you can get of yourself on how you need to change to lead change can be obtained on-line. There is a self-perception (i.e. your view of yourself) Leadership HealthCheck which you can access at PentacleTheVBS.com/Healthchecks.

This leadership healthcheck will, if you are honest and have insight into how you *really* lead, tell you what your followers actually **receive** from your leadership.

We can always inject some reality into your self-assessment by organising for your team and stakeholders to score you on the same parameters.

Just click the link *"Stakeholder Feedback please"* on the response.

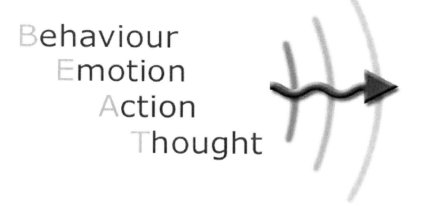

The truth is you'll probably need to re-assess your BEAT. That is the <u>Behaviours</u> you demonstrate, the <u>Emotions</u> you express, the <u>Actions</u> you carry out and the <u>Thoughts</u> you share.

CHAPTER 8 WHAT DO I NEED TO UNDERSTAND ABOUT BEHAVIOUR?

In which you learn why
"behaviour is your saviour"

To know what people really think pay regard to what
they do, rather than what they say.
Rene Descartes

For the last decade 'behaviour' has been chic. It's almost impossible to walk past a human resources or learning & development professional without hearing the words, "but it all comes down to real changes in behaviour." With that constant use of the "B" word you'd imagine that not only would it be easy to understand but also to define.

You're in a meeting. Suddenly, unexpectedly your boss's boss's boss strolls into the room and sits down, obviously keen to join in the discussion. What happens? Did you notice everyone's posture change slightly? Did you notice the accents become more or less pronounced? People who, 'till now, had been silent becoming animated and talkative? What you are observing is behaviour change. In a work context we're likely to have learnt behaviours we think are effective or work well in these public scenarios.

*Later, at home with friends, you are describing the unexpected visit. There is laugher as you mimic or parody what occurred. You're relaxed and we are seeing different behaviour. Behaviour closer to the **real you,** the relaxed you, in a safe environment with friends. You can relax with friends because you know that they aren't judging you. It's really common that your friends share many of your attitudes; perhaps that's why they're friends. They dislike pomposity as much as you do. Their attitudes, like yours, are influenced by what they believe. We all have a hierarchy of beliefs which we hold really dear. You probably believe pompous people are show-offs and shallow and on your hierarchy of "things you really believe in", your values, those two things, pomposity and showing-off rank high in your list of NoNo's.*

But how did these values get onto your list? Chances are you adopted them from someone else - probably your parents. You see, the things which drive you were often implanted deep in your subconscious during your formative years. In silences most of us can still hear our parent's voices. These drivers may be underpinned by something else you've absorbed in your subconscious.

You see, if you take a human being and you slice them across the middle of their being you discover that they are many layered, like an onion.

The Human Onion

BEHAVIOUR (PUBLIC)
BEHAVIOUR (PRIVATE)
ATTITUDES
VALUES
DRIVERS
EGO

what 'they' see
when they observe you

In the centre are all the subconscious bits, **ego, id** etc. Around that are primary **drivers** - many of the things you heard or experienced at a very early formative age. You hear your parent's voices saying, "be good", "be strong", "I wish you wouldn't get drunk", "don't be such a control freak" (the last two were probably not directed at you).

The next ring represents your **values** - the things you believe, which influence your attitudes to what you do and what happens around you. Your **attitudes** influence your **behaviour**. Behaviour works at two levels, **private** behaviour (the **'real you'**) and **public** behaviour (you in a social context - remember your colleagues sitting up and speaking out!).

One of my favourite video clips, found on the web, is a 30 second section that shows a robot walking, interacting with humans, shaking hands and generally carrying out a discourse. What is amazing is that it looks so alive, so human and perhaps more importantly it looks like a nice, friendly guy! How does that work? Well, it seems as if the gestures that have been programmed in, the head nodding - held tilted slightly to one side, the slight bowing demonstrating deference and avoiding aggression is why the robot (which remember is neither alive nor a human being) comes across as a nice person.

What this example tells us is **that people observe and engage with your behaviour, NOT your personality**. As a leader this is a crucial thing to understand. It is not your intentions or your warm heartedness that we observe but simply the behaviour you demonstrate - Think of Al Gore before the US elections - public behaviour = robot. After failure - public behaviour = friendly, favourite uncle. Had he changed personality? No, just behaviour and that is why at Pentacle we give very "short shrift" to personality tests and psychometrics, because what happens to matter most in leadership is your ability to engage with followers and that is about behaviours.

The secret is that people follow a leader's behaviour far more than what they say. How often have you seen the political no hoper speaking in a flat voice with no physical gestures explaining 'how very, very excited she is to have this huge, amazing opportunity!'

CHAPTER 9 WHAT DO I NEED TO DO ABOUT MY BEHAVIOUR?

In which you learn how to behave to encourage followers

Question: How can you figure out how to behave to encourage followers?

Answer   Pretend to be a follower and ask yourself what you would be looking for

Obeng

Here are a couple of scenarios. Do you think the 'leader' is being effective?   Which other behaviour do you think would work better?

A) *It's a bit stressful. For a start the move into Russia means understanding the dynamics of a completely new market. It's obvious that there is a huge opportunity and yet... Everyone is using the word 'opportunity' and you suspect it's because they haven't really worked out what success will look like. Is it sales? Establishing a joint venture? Having a bigger market presence than your key competitors? Or not getting hassled by the local 'Mafia'? You have no idea of the best way to approach exploiting the opportunity and* *you're not sure anyone else does either. This is the second time it's been tried. The first time the entire team were made redundant after three months and now you've been asked to be part of the new team. Jed who is supposed to be leading it has now had two meetings. At the first he spent the whole time standing, waving his arms about and telling us how famous we would be once we made a success of the move to Russia. He said he was 100% committed to the project and would even be moving his family over. He said he was completely behind us and would give us all the support we needed.*

B) *It's the fifth year of the annual office dragon-boat race. A combined picnic by the river, boat race, and disco for 400 people. After an initially rocky start five years ago it now works very smoothly. The staff now like the consistency of the event and the informal nature. The organising team has remained the same over the five year period except for the new committee chairman this year. They all say that the project really is a dream to work on and amazing that, with so little impact on their personal time, they can put on a great event year after year. It's just that everyone knows their role and contribution to getting it set up and what to do on the day. But now the new committee chairman wants to have planning meetings and a team building event. Unusually for us he'd called a meeting. At that meeting he* *was very friendly indeed and went round shaking hands and smiling. He asked us, <u>all</u> the team, to introduce ourselves and to say why we enjoy being part of the team. Then he asked us for ideas on what could be done differently. That part was embarrassing, the answers were garbled. It was clear no one had thought about that - we are all quite happy with how things are now. He sat down on the floor at this point with his palms outstretched like an Indian guru. Now he wants weekly sharing of information and updates to each other on what's happening and a discussion on what the team is learning, what is going well and what is not going well...*

Selecting the wrong behaviour in each situation is likely to lead to failure. Someone who had led several 'Painting-by-Numbers' type projects would probably have created a set of habits and behaviours for leading people in that situation. When presented with a 'Lost in the Fog' type of project - the same structured, ordered and directive behaviours which work in the 'Painting-by-Numbers' situation are completely inappropriate.

Below are four lists of behaviours (personal activities) - sometimes they are difficult to separate. Which set of behaviours do you think will give the leaders the best chance of success in the four change filters (situations)?

- Being Lost in the Fog (unclear goal and means)

- Going on a Quest (clear goal but unclear means)

- Making a Movie (pre-defined means but unclear goal)

- Painting by Numbers (clear goals and method)

The answers are at the end of the Chapter

Demonstrate experience
Demonstrate a track record

Clearly communicate the goals
Set challenging standards
Resolve conflicts and boundary issues
Be firm but fair in dealing with people/ associates

Define the boundaries between the tasks
Assign tasks
Organise
Plan activities for the whole team

Clearly define goals
Know and understand the methods and techniques employed

1

2

Demonstrate courage
Encapsulate the solution to the problem in a persuasive manner
Live the values embodied in the project

Communicate the vision enthusiastically and persuasively
Must be single minded (almost to the point of obstinacy)
Gain personal ownership for the idea from other people/ associates
Show genuine concern for team members
Encourage sharing of learning
Maintain the vision and its importance in the light of short term failure

---

Be almost obsessive about high quality standards
Motivate through relationships

Set challenging personal visions for your people/ associates
Provide space for creativity in line with the vision

Make sure that the team all understand how their role contributes
Review progress against the vision
Find opportunities for your people/ associates to use their skills to the fullest
Keep the use of the methodology as far in the background as possible
without de motivating the team
Be prepared to adjust or modify the initial goals as further objectives are identified

Be persistent in listening - in order to be clear on what success looks like
Hold a steady vision for long periods of time
Build a vision of the project goals from stakeholder aspirations

3

Demonstrate calmness (even when panicking)
Communicate widely and effectively
Clearly articulate a vision (usually the opposite of the problem faced)
Show genuine concern for the team
Proceed one step at a time
Be creative with any new opportunities or insights which present themselves
Praise initiative taken by the team
Build trust Make promises and keep them
Accept offers of ideas and efforts from your people/ associates
Encourage the team to communicate amongst themselves
Capture any learning the team makes
Involve your people/associates up front and in decision making
Ensure ownership
Describe and capture the nature of the problem faced
Provide intellectual challenge through questioning
Be prepared to go to others (match and lead)
Listen effectively to both logical and emotional concerns

4

Now see if you can guess which behaviour set would be most effective in Scenario A.

Go back and re-read the scenario. Now a bit of 'role play': Pretend that you are one of the potential followers. What do you think would encourage you to follow?

Have another go. This time try Scenario B

The answers are on the next page..

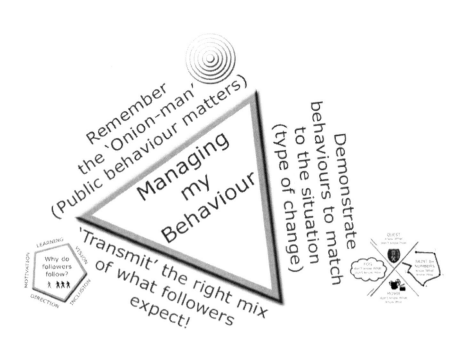

Answers

1. Painting by Numbers (clear goals and method)?
2. Going on a Quest (clear goal but unclear means)
3. Making a Movie (pre-defined means but unclear goal)
4. Being Lost in the Fog (unclear goal and means)

Did you get them right?

More importantly did you realise...

	The Leader Transmitted	The Situation Requested (Filter)	Followers Expected
Scenario A	Pioneer behaviours Set 2 (Quest)	Innovator behaviours Set 4 (Fog)	V L D I M
Scenario B	Innovator behaviours Set 4 (Fog)	Adapter behaviour Set 1 (Painting by numbers)	V M D I L

Vision - Learning - Direction - Inclusion - Motivation

CHAPTER 10 WHAT DO I NEED TO UNDERSTAND ABOUT EMOTIONS?

In which you learn how emotions influence the success of leadership

Feelings are not supposed to be logical. Dangerous is the man who has rationalized his emotions.

David Borenstein

The first and most important thing you need to understand about **emotions** is that they **are the key indicator of whether or not you have followers**. <u>**Listen to them carefully**</u>. If you know that there are people who are supposed to be following you and you're scared that you will let them down you probably have followers. That feeling is an indicator of a 'connection' between you and them. If you have no concerns of letting people down, then you may think you're leading but there probably isn't anyone following!

It's a surprise to you. You hadn't seen it coming. How could they, out of the blue, change what had already been agreed and on top of that insist on such a 'stupid' set of new deliverables? You tried to argue your case but for some reason you found you weren't as articulate and erudite as usual. You could barely string a sentence together. If truth be told you're livid. You stomp back to your desk, shoulders hunched. Other people might describe you as sulking, but you don't see it that way. To you, your behaviour is 100% justified. You have five minutes before the weekly team update - you burn those in a fury. At the team meeting you brood darkly. When it comes to your turn you let them have it - after all it's not your fault. You tell it as it is, placing the blame fairly and squarely where it belongs. You begin by saying "I've been told to tell you..." The mood of the meeting deteriorates...

So why are you in such a bad mood? And why do you think you have to infect everyone else with it? You are in a bad mood **because you have absolutely no immediate control over the way you react to unexpected change**. It's hard wired into your brain. All human beings have this response however sophisticated or intelligent they are.

Now do you understand why you were speechless? This response is present in every human being and since most of the people I know are human beings it is important to be aware of it. From your point of view as a leader it is crucial you understand the effect others can have on you through surprising change. The reason it's crucial is because in the example above the leader simply passes it on, infecting the rest of the team with 'negative vibes'. So why does the leader pass on the negativity? I don't really know. Perhaps it is some misguided view of revenge on the person who upset them? What you have to understand about emotions is that they are yours first and then other people's next and the reason for that is that **emotions are infectious**.

Do you have a friend with a strange, boring looking hobby you don't share? Something like fishing? You imagine it will be a bad experience but your friend loves it and is so energised and enthusiastic about it that you become convinced that it can't really be as bad as you imagine. So one day you accept their offer of going fishing with them. You're up before dawn, wet, cold and yes you discover it is even worse than you initially imagined.

So what made you go fishing with them? Quite simply their emotion infected you. You saw their face light up as they talked about the sun glistening on the rippling stream and you heard the modulation in their voice. And that is why you went. Emotions are infectious and are easily caught. The leader in our first example hasn't understood this. If someone else takes you by surprise and triggers your fight/freeze/flee sub-routine you need to recover and manage your emotion so you don't transmit it to others.

It is crucial that you remain alert to the emotions of your potential followers. It's easy. Open yourself up and empathise - you'll soon get the 'temperature'!

Many leaders do not understand the importance of managing their own emotions. I've met people who feel happy when the project is on track and desperately miserable when it isn't and let it show. I've met people who feel happy when the weather is good and miserable when it isn't. If you don't manage your emotions, something or someone else is going to do it for you. And you won't like the consequences.

Have you ever had the experience where with the radio and TV off and in a moment of contemplation you hear voices. No I don't mean those sort of voices, I mean you hear your own voice talking to you. It usually uses the name your most critical parent used to call you by and says things to you like

"So you think you're going to get away with taking on that project and make a success of it? Well you won't. You'll probably fail. You always fail. Do you remember what a fool you made of yourself in Mr. William's class? That time too you thought you'd get away with it but you didn't. You're completely useless..."

If you have any good sense you start singing to your self loudly or turn the radio back on. The truth is you often have conversations with yourself and for most of us the conversation is not the most energising and uplifting we can imagine. In fact, it's usually pretty damning and debilitating!

You're probably thinking that this is a good thing. Nothing like a dose of cold reality to stiffen the spine and make you aware of the challenges ahead. Unfortunately this negative internal conversation has an enormous downside for a Perfect Leader.

You know how sometimes when you are really excited and keen to get something done it doesn't feel like work? How does that work?

Have you ever had to learn a new game or skill? I remember being given the game Blokus as a Christmas present. By fluke I won the first game but the boost in confidence that gave me meant that for the rest of that evening I was unbeatable. When you are learning something new and it's going well you have all the energy you need and can't seem to put a foot wrong? Do you have any idea why that happens?

The reason is that your body listens to the conversations you have with yourself and uses them as a cue to how much effort to put into things. This happens even if you don't really believe what you are saying to yourself!

You wake up saying to yourself "I just can't wait to get started," and your body senses this and it can't wait to get started. You win the game and tell yourself "I'm very good at this," and your body knows to stay alert to make sure that you really do play brilliantly.

And that is why your negative conversations are so dreadful. They drain your energy and will. They make it much more likely that you will fail thus fulfilling the negative prophesy!

Argue your limitations and you get to keep them

Richard Bach

Managing your emotions is intensely difficult but is a crucial skill for a Complete Leader.

It really is brilliant, even though you say so yourself and it's your idea. So you can't wait to share it with the team. It's exciting, fragile and beautiful. If you can make this baby work it will solve everything. So you take this lovely 'baby' to the next team meeting and ten minutes into the meeting you take it out and show it to everyone. You explain your idea in a measured but excited way. You were expecting applause. Instead they fold their arms. You explain how beautiful the baby is. One of the team retorts "It's ugly" What a shock! You obviously haven't explained it clearly enough, so you elaborate. Highlighting the beautiful baby eyes. "No'" says another, "that's definitely the ugliest baby I've ever seen!" The argument continues, "My baby is beautiful" - "No, it's ugly." Then one team member steps in and says. "You know, what you're describing is a bit like an idea I had myself last month. I'd be happy to help you develop it" (in other words "your baby looks like my baby. I'll help you bring it up!"). But for everyone else they leave the team meeting and do <u>nothing</u> different as a result of your idea.

The EUREKA Syndrome

You see, the problem is that there isanother response hard-wired into your brain. You are 'programmed' to be controlled by questions (or other inquiring stimuli).

It is the combination of these two hard wired responses, pushing back against imposed change and becoming excited about self-created change which lead to the **Third Law of Change**:

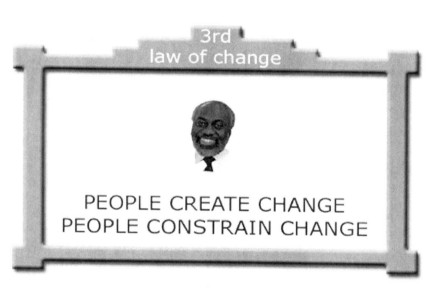

3rd law of change

PEOPLE CREATE CHANGE
PEOPLE CONSTRAIN CHANGE

As a Complete Leader you should probably have this Law tattooed somewhere you will see it often. **If you engage them they will go to the ends of the earth to make it happen. If you shock them (i.e. surprise them) they will resist the change until they die!**

CHAPTER 11 WHAT DO I NEED TO DO ABOUT MY EMOTIONS?

In which you learn how to control your internal emotions and guide your projected emotions

The degree of one's emotion varies inversely with ones knowledge of the facts

Bertrand Russell

It's going just as badly as you thought it would. You weren't expecting the project manager to make that comment from in front of the CEO and you handled it badly, over-reacting and lashing out when you got back to your team. It's cold, wet and grey outside so you're feeling really miserable. You're slumped over your desk, shoulders hunched, chin below your navel. The corners of your mouth are turned down so far you look like a negative smiley :-("It's not fair," you think, but the voice in your head says "I knew you'd never make it. Pretending to be a competent manager when you don't have the background or training". "But I have been trained," you reply, struggling for control. "Yes," the voice counters, "but what a poor trainer he was. And the course was so boring, you didn't learn a thing. All you have is a pointless certificate. You hoped you could use your accreditation to bluff your way through, to make people think that you actually know something about management". You shrug defeatedly. "Yes," says the voice, "and this isn't the first time you've made a mess of things". By now your self-esteem has gone on a two week holiday. You'll stand no chance of leading or influencing effectively and perhaps, just for now, you might not even try.

Leading change is tough. Thank goodness! If it wasn't tough anyone could do it and your salary would be even lower than it is!

Because it's tough, as a Leader, you need all the emotional strength and resource you can muster behind you. The problem is that often we can be our own worst enemy. We do this by not fully understanding how our minds and emotions work and instead of harnessing them we let them run riot.

It's cold, wet and grey so you're feeling miserable.

It doesn't help that the forecasters refer to rain and wind as 'bad weather' - it's not bad weather. It's just another, different type of weather. It's good weather for the plants, for clearing the air of pollution etc. True you could be suffering from S.A.D. syndrome or be low on vitamin D - but chances are you aren't. You're just taking the lazy route in managing your emotions. This route has been described as **out-sourcing management of your emotions to the weather**.

You're slumped over your desk, shoulders hunched, chin below your navel.

The corners of your mouth are turned down so far you look like a negative smiley :-(

Your posture significantly influences your emotions. Try sitting upright, pulling your shoulder blades together (not puffing out your chest), raising your chin and putting a large sloppy smile on your face without giggling out loud. Try walking whilst swinging your arms more energetically than is absolutely necessary. I call these physical changes GoofMicking^{TM} I want you to think about combining Goofy's long stride arm-swinging walk with Mickey Mouse's silly smile! Try these and take back control of your life from the rain.

Think, who you would rather follow in most situations - a downbeat, gloom & doom merchant or a quietly confident leader.

You weren't expecting the project manager to make that comment from in front of the CEO and you handled it badly, over-reacting and lashing out when you got back to your team.

And be sure to make time to recover from emotional shocks before 'kicking the cat'. Everyone needs a warm quiet place to hide in order to calm down. In your diary try to have time allocated to 'Project Blue,[9]' an opportunity to 'hide' until you get your "emotional" act together. If you have a good friend take advantage of their friendship and let them cocoon you!

...but the voice in your head says "I knew you'd never make it".

---

[9] I learnt this name from a participant who remarked after I had made this point that he called this space and time Project Blue!

Most (normal) people talk to themselves (the others have an invisible parrot on their right shoulder talking to them) . Not out loud but secretly inside. Do you? It has two useful functions - it **tells our bodies how to behave next** and, as part of our internal knowledge management system, it acts as a **voice-enabled,** Google **search engine**.

I have a demonstration I use to help people to understand that simply saying something negative and derogatory about yourself to your self can sap all your resolve. I choose a large strapping bloke from the audience. I do a strength test - say, me pushing against his hand. I then get him to repeat a negative phrase such as "I am weak and deserve to fail in all I do!" a number of times over and then repeat the strength test - which he fails. It's not whether you believe what your voice says that matters, it's the fact that it **tells your body how to behave next.** You need to learn a technique I call PlusVibes™. You will find life much easier if you learn and create several positive <u>present</u> tense statements you can repeat to yourself when the going gets tough, such as "I'm effective and confident in leading others to achieve our goals". My favourite is "I'm moving steadily towards my goals **one step at a time!"**

"...the session was so boring!"

In our new reality unfortunately the pace of change has outstripped the ability of many of us and our organisations to learn. What this means is that although in the past your trainer had a 95% understanding of what you most needed to learn, in the NewWorld, your trainer doesn't. So **<u>you</u>** have to take a lot of the responsibility for **what** you learn and **how** you put it into practice. You have to actively participate and not just sit receptive like a piece of blank cardboard waiting to be entertained. A useless and boring session in the NewWorld is jointly created by a useless and boring trainer and useless and boring participants - you!

"... All you have is a pointless certificate".

This I cannot help you with. Serves you right for wasting a week of your life on OldWorld stuff!

"...and this isn't the first time you've made a mess of things".

It's your **voice enabled** Google **search engine** kicking in. It feeds up automatically the answers to the questions you've asked. You've asked it the wrong question. You've asked it to do an on-line search for past disasters so you can avoid obvious errors. Why not do a search for 'past successes'?

Once you have this mastered the last part is to immunise yourself to surprises and the emotional freeze they bring with them. I use a technique called HorrorScope^{TM}. Quite simply as you travel to work take some time to brainstorm the surprises that might hit you. Your PA unexpectedly hands in their notice. The fire alarm interrupts your crucial presentation to your director, you arrive to discover the business has been the victim of a hostile bid.

Feel the event and allow your heart rate and breathing to rise as they probably will. Then start to **imagine the events which would follow** as you calmed down and again took control of the situation.

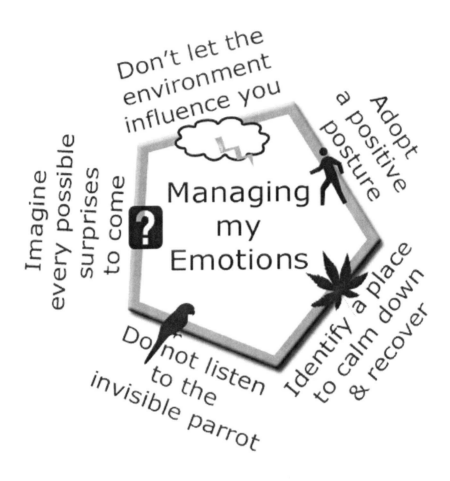

CHAPTER 12 WHAT DO I NEED TO UNDERSTAND ABOUT ACTIONS?

In which you learn how to select the best actions

> Better have 2 dummies acting
> than 3 intellectuals talking
> *Chris Waistcoat*

As I write this there are floods in the UK. Floods to wash-in a new government. The media are in a frenzy and one of the questions is "Should the new PM visit the flooded areas?" Well should he? The answer of course is that it depends. For a leader talking about a 'break with the past' he probably should since it is exactly the sort of action his predecessor would never have taken. People listen to what you say but watch your behaviour for clues about what you really think. People watch how you behave but observe your actions to decide what you really value.

Historians write about actions. Finally it is through actions that the leader (you) delivers change. So it is true you "must act" (in the words of George W Bush) - but **not just any action**. Acting because you feel "something must be done" is how you could end up a mis-leader. Before anything else, you must remember the fourth new world rule (see Chapter 14) **DO NOTHING OF NO USE!** If

[12] ***Putting Strategy to Work!*** *The Blueprint for Transforming Ideas into Action -* *Eddie Obeng* - Financial Times ISBN 0273602659

followers perceive that your actions are pointless or futile they are less likely to follow you!

How do I choose between actions?

The quarter has just ended and it's looking bad. You've missed the numbers by miles. The competitors have eaten your lunch. They're smaller, they're growing and they have a more up-to-date and customer-friendly product line than yours. You blame the sales force. They're just not trying hard enough. Something must be done. You're unhappy but not despondent because you have a plan. You've just read about how GE used a traffic light system to focus its sales force on selling and you intend to implement that idea. It's either that or find out what can be done about the product line to make it more customer friendly. But that could take a long time and isn't in your hands. It will require difficult, heavily political cross-functional work. There's no guarantee it will work and anyway it doesn't solve the immediate problem.

You pitch your idea to your line director and the HR Director and get a thumbs-up. Now you get the sales team together and you give them the news. The "I am excited about the challenge" speech. You say, "It gives each person an opportunity to prove themselves" and you use several other great inspirational phrases you've come across. The upshot is everyone starts with their personal rating at green. Miss your first month's target you go amber. Miss your second month's target you go red.   After red you go home and don't come back.   Starting the month it looks great.   The forecasts are up much higher than you had hoped. Mid-month the actual numbers lag but there seem to be a lot more prospects in the pipeline.   End of the month and now there is a spattering of amber.   But the forecasts still look good and the sales guys keep stopping you in the corridor with stories of more new prospects. You have a team pep talk to remind them of the carrot of the bonus and the stick of what happens after a red. The mood is upbeat. Month three is a "redwash".   Two days later you arrive in your office to discover your desk littered with resignation letters from a third of the sales team. Now it's the end of the month. A third of your team have left - amazingly they have found jobs immediately with competitors.   They must have gone for interviews almost as soon as they reached amber! It is the worst quarter ever and with the team under-resourced by a third, you suspect that the next quarter will also be a dog.

As a leader you are **leading to the future**. Mis-leaders get dazzled by current irritations. In *Putting Strategy to Work*[12] we explained how strategic leaders approach decisions. As a Complete Leader when you make a decision you **go into the future to see how it turns out**. You consider how it affects other people and how they are likely to react. You look at the options that their response leaves you and check that the future outcome will be in line with the vision and not carry so many unintended consequences it would have been better to do nothing! You solve today's problem AND you solve tomorrow's.

The first challenge is to understand what the ISSUE actually is. In the example above it looks as if the issue is about missing or achieving the sales figures. Leadership decisions are rarely that simple. The real issue is how do you maintain the viability of the organisation whilst a more customer friendly product line is developed? How do you get past the difficult cross functional issues? That needs leadership. That means you.

The next thing which trips a leader up is looking for STAKEHOLDERS in the wrong place. Most look up. In the scenario you did too - your Line Director and HR Director. But by missing the sales team as co-creators of the short term solution you were about to lose your following.

You took an off-the-shelf solution and applied it to your problem, but what did you really WANT as an outcome?

And did you look at enough options? Engaging the sales team might have generated some different OPTIONS.

And finally, once you had selected your preferred option you forgot to go into the future and test it. You forgot to ask your self "If I choose this what happens NEXT?"

ISWON is the tongue mangling acronym we've developed for this leader's decision making process. (pronounced He's Won! - not completely gender neutral but hopefully memorable)

Are you an Action man? a James Bond? Are your gadgets more important to you than air and water? Are you addicted to your phone and Blackberry as if it were a tamagochi? Do you respond instantly to every text message without thinking about the futurity of it?

Remember, "It's not because it's urgent that it's important!" and "Act in haste, suffer at your leisure!"

CHAPTER 13 WHAT DO I NEED TO DO ABOUT MY ACTIONS?

In which you learn how to identify
and develop the best actions

Actions speak louder than words
but not nearly as often!

Mark Twain

The key is to establish the most appropriate set of actions. Sounds obvious? But how do you do that when you face, for example, **'Foggy** change' (that is the change which in Chapter 5 made you feel frightened, embarrassed, confused and concerned). Because you have little clue of what exactly will be delivered or how difficult it will be, you l may thinking that "something needs to be done." But will it be worth it? Will your effort at least be matched by the returns? **You need a short 'Business case'!**

The tool we use is called the GapLeap™ It is described in detail in *Perfect Projects*[13] so we will only give an overview here. It is

What IF NOT FIXED ...   What IF FIXED ...

< Gap >

WHY NOT FIXED YET

---

[13] Perfect Projects E Obeng 2003 Pentacle Works

15

based on a very simple template and uses 'post it'/sticky notes.

Stage 1

< Gap >   Our level of
           innovation
           is too low

Define the gap you have to leap. This is written as a sentence describing the difference between the current situation and the way you would like it to be. Do it with your stakeholders and agree on a common formulation. This phase is very important in order to engage them.

Stage 2

What IF NOT FIXED ...

Sales decline
will continue
5% p.annum

Our products
will be less
competitive

We'll have
fewer product
on the Mkt

We'll get
bought up

We'll have
to increase
Mktg budget

Brainstorm together using post-its all the things which are happening or will happen if the 'gap' is not leapt (IF NOT FIXED). Give people enough time to prepare their post-its. When posting them on the template, make sure that they are shared with everyone. (Read them out loud)

Stage 3

What IF FIXED ...

Profits will
recover 2%
next year

Revenue will
grow

Customer
satisfaction
will increase

Staff attrition
will diminish

Comms
budgets will
decrease

We'll be able
to recruit
more staff

Brainstorm together using post-its all the things which are happening or will happen if the 'gap' is leapt (IF FIXED). Make sure you explore all dimensions of the issue and do not exclude possible negative impacts. Post these up, reading out loud.

Now review what you have posted so far on both sides and agree if the gap is serious and significant enough to continue to working on it.

Stage 4

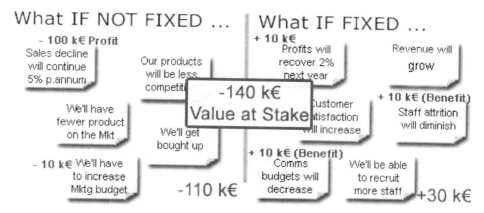

What IF NOT FIXED ...   What IF FIXED ...

- 100 k€ Profit
Sales decline will continue 5% p.annum

Our products will be less competiti

We'll have fewer product on the Mkt

We'll get bought up

- 10 k€ We'll have to increase Mktg budget

-110 k€

-140 k€
Value at Stake

+ 10 k€
Profits will recover 2% next year

Customer satisfaction will increase

+ 10 k€ (Benefit)
Comms budgets will decrease

Revenue will grow

+ 10 k€ (Benefit)
Staff attrition will diminish

We'll be able to recruit more staff +30 k€

Now quantify the impact of this gap. (This will be particularly important later for convincing your followers and stakeholders to act). Select a reasonable time period. Estimate the financial impact of each post-it over this period. Add up the financial amounts. It is important not to double count! You should end up with two figures - The monetary impact of doing nothing (...IF NOT FIXED), The monetary impact of doing something (...IF FIXED).

The sum of the benefits of leaping the gap is called the **"Value at Stake"** If this VaS is high enough, you can go on to Stage 5

Stage 5

Answer the question 'If this is so valuable WHY have we NOT FIXED it YET?

WHY NOT FIXED YET

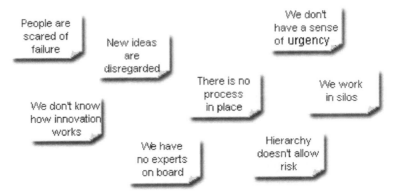

Brainstorming with post-its again. Again make sure you read out loud what is posted. You now have the full scope of all the actions you could take to leap the gap.

Stage 6

WHY NOT FIXED YET

The raw material to start designing a rational plan ...

Cluster and shuffle the post-its in the bottom WHY NOT FIXED YET? section around so that the ones furthest to the **left** are those that promise **biggest benefit** or the **least effort**.

To the **right**, place the ones with the **least benefit** or which will require the **most effort**.

Stage 7

Decide which actions you intend to take and estimate the financial impact of each post it you intend to take action on. Calculate a total. The business case for your change is approximately the

Value at Stake (adjusted to match the extent to which you feel your actions will leap the gap) divided by the total cost of the post-its in the bottom section divided by the time period you selected.

Now you have your actions (each post-it can be read as a corrective action) prioritised.

You have the financials for a business case and the post-its provide the narrative. But don't rush them and **don't overfill your diary with actions** (67% of your time is the magic figure ;-) The reason in the words of Harold Wilson is "Events, dear boy, events". Unless you leave sufficient time to think and time for additional actions as life unravels you will find yourself unable to cope. One step at a time!

What do I do if the actions themselves are 'foggy' and I'm unsure of precisely what to do or how to do it?

For this you need to take some StickySteps ™. In *All Change* [15] the StickyStep™ technique is explained in great detail for real planners. As a leader all you need is the shortened version.

Stage 1

Select an action from your GapLeap and make it a "positive action" (e.g. *We do not have a sense of emergency* becomes *Make our people understand the emergency*)

Stage 2

Pretend you've finished successfully delivering this action. You are now six months in the future reflecting on your success. Bask in the glory. How does it feel? What do you hear people saying? How do things look? Now we are going to reminisce and remember the way we got here.

Stage 3

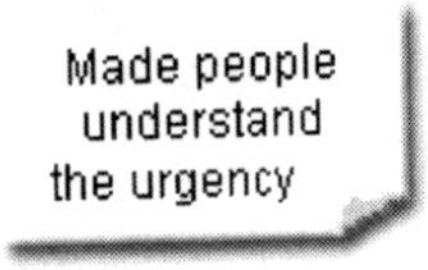

Made people
understand
the urgency

Write up your positive action on a post-it.

From now on every post-it you write **MUST START WITH A VERB (DOING WORD) IN THE PAST TENSE AND MUST BE A COMPLETE SENTENCE**

Stage 4

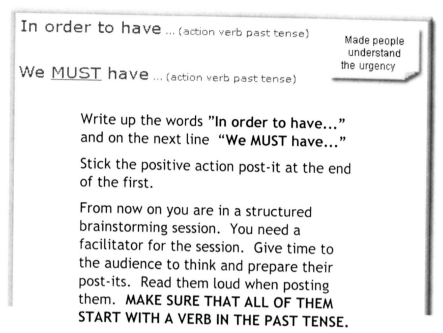

In order to have ... (action verb past tense)

Made people understand the urgency

We **MUST** have ... (action verb past tense)

Write up the words **"In order to have..."** and on the next line **"We MUST have..."**

Stick the positive action post-it at the end of the first.

From now on you are in a structured brainstorming session. You need a facilitator for the session. Give time to the audience to think and prepare their post-its. Read them loud when posting them. **MAKE SURE THAT ALL OF THEM START WITH A VERB IN THE PAST TENSE.**

Stage 5

We **MUST** have ... (action verb past tense)

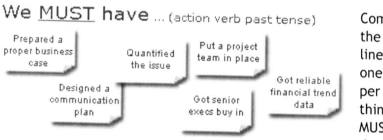

Prepared a proper business case

Quantified the issue

Put a project team in place

Designed a communication plan

Got senior execs buy in

Got reliable financial trend data

Complete the second line using one post-it per idea of things you MUST have done

Each one must make a complete sentence (for example, In order to have made people understand the emergency we must have prepared a proper business case.) You must have no missed or extra words.

Stage 6

Shuffle the post-its into a timeline.

We **MUST** have ... (action verb past tense)

Sequence:
Earlyish --> Lateish   (standard focus)
Easy --> Hard   (credibility focus)
Engaging Stakeholders --> Mixed (involvement focus)

Stage 7

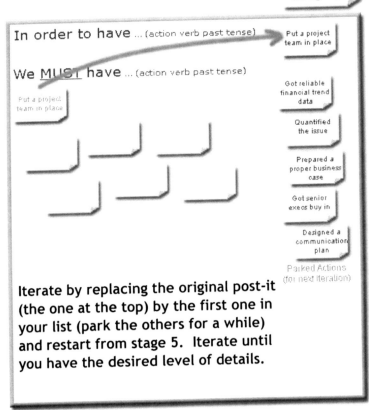

Iterate by replacing the original post-it
(the one at the top) by the first one in
your list (park the others for a while)
and restart from stage 5. Iterate until
you have the desired level of details.

Stage 8

Schedule the concrete tasks on a timeline

Make sure you know who is helping you to do what

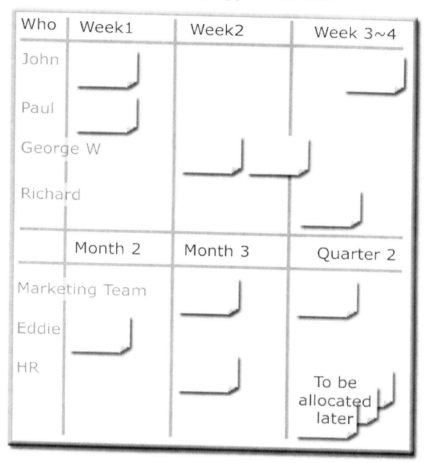

Who	Week1	Week2	Week 3~4
John			
Paul			
George W			
Richard			
	Month 2	Month 3	Quarter 2
Marketing Team			
Eddie			
HR			To be allocated later

You now have a concrete plan, out of the fog!

Repeat the process with your key followers or stakeholders in order to engage them.

CHAPTER 14 WHAT DO I NEED TO UNDERSTAND ABOUT MY THINKING?

In which you learn what to change about how we think in the New World.

> I think therefore I am
> *Descartes*
> I think therefore they should follow
> *Anon.*

It doesn't seem to matter how quickly you reply to messages on your Blackberry they just keep building up. Thank God it's almost Christmas because as we all know Christmas is 'the amnesty.' People return brainwashed.

Can I ask a very challenging question? "How much of your work time is futile? I mean completely wasted? 10%? 20 %? No, I mean really wasted. If you audited your actions and decisions a year after they'd been carried out or made, how much would they be worth? OK, if you wish to scrape the barrel you can even add to the value the impact of the actions and decisions that would have happened with the 'Do Nothing' option. 40%? 50%?"

The only scientific data I have is from a diary exercise. I had managers of a client organisation keep a diary on a spreadsheet of what they were doing minute by minute (in three minute blocks) for a week (by the way, doing this well is really tough). Then we waited four months and asked whether each activity had indeed improved the bottom line or made their personal life-experience better. Do you know what the average wasted time was? 85%!

Why did this happen? They weren't particularly incompetent or below average (only 50% of people are below average!). It's just that each day they either chose to or were compelled to do things and think in what we call the 'OldWorld' way, using concepts, tools, techniques and behaviours that were cutting edge in a previous century but are counter productive now. For example, they would travel for an hour to attend a one hour meeting, sit in the room, have a good discussion, scribble personal notes of the meeting in red and black notebooks, and agree a date for the next meeting and then travel back.

They could instead have worked virtually via a phone conference managed on a strict rotation basis (no secret emailing during the call). Structuring the issues using a BubbleDiagram^{TM}, making notes and capturing actions live on a shared screen and directly into a collaborative webspace.

- And since working virtually for more than 45 minutes is difficult the meeting would have been 25% shorter.

This approach would have captured all the learning for the people who missed it and for future reference and would have followed a Performance Enhancement Tool (PETs^{TM}) framework, so the discussion would have been comprehensive.

- And since people would see actions going up against their names they would be compelled to act.

- And since the minutes of the meeting were shared 'live' people could confirm understanding or challenge the actions immediately.

So...

• Productivity increase 300%
• Engagement and commitment up.
• Clarity of actions, decisions and delivery and engagement in next steps - Up!

So why do we persist with the out-moded way of doing things? I don't. So I guess **you** need to answer that.

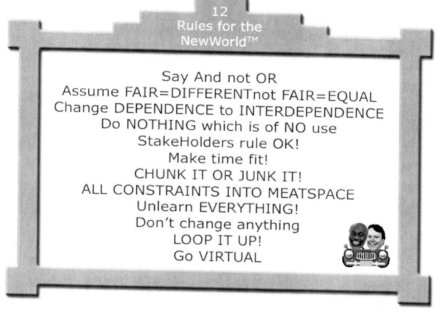

12
Rules for the
NewWorld™

Say And not OR
Assume FAIR=DIFFERENTnot FAIR=EQUAL
Change DEPENDENCE to INTERDEPENDENCE
Do NOTHING which is of NO use
StakeHolders rule OK!
Make time fit!
CHUNK IT OR JUNK IT!
ALL CONSTRAINTS INTO MEATSPACE
Unlearn EVERYTHING!
Don't change anything
LOOP IT UP!
Go VIRTUAL

One main reason is that our thinking is not keeping up with the times. In *New Rules for the New World*[17] I identified 12 common thinking mistakes people make. I learnt this by spending years trying to understand why even with brilliant

---

[17] *New Rules for the New World* Eddie Obeng - Wiley ISBN 1900961156

NewWorld intentions organisations and individuals still ended up with results they didn't want.

Here is a brief summary

1. Say 'AND!' not 'OR'
    Bust paradoxes by rejecting
    the traditional 'OR thinking'
    pattern
2. Assume FAIR = DIFFERENT
not FAIR = EQUAL
    Develop more styles
    Learn to communicate
    Purpose
3. Change DEPENDENCE
to INTERDEPENDENCE
    Split Accountability from
    Responsibility
    Bet on teams and networks
    and the individual
4. Do NOTHING
which is of NO use
    Show me the money!
    Focus!
    DO IT ONCE
5. Stakeholders rule OK!
    Know your stakeholders.
    Trust first, then Tit-for-tat.
    Some suppliers more
    important than some
    customers.
    Delight and Challenge the
    people you work with.

6. Make time fit
    Make TIME = PARALLEL
    Everything has sell-by dates.
    Do it Now!
7. CHUNK IT OR JUNK IT!
    Modularize!
    Make it self similar.
    Review too often!
8. ALL CONSTRAINTS
INTO MEAT SPACE
    Re-invent your information.
    Stay DIGITAL in cyberspace.
    Stop communicating!
9. Unlearn EVERYTHING!
    Every group a culture.
    Only learn what others don't
    know!
10. Don't change anything!
    Beware the LAWS OF
    CHANGE.
    Respond with Awesome
    Velocity and Seize the
    Future, Now!
    Robust or Bust.
11. LOOP IT UP!
    Form - virtual - loops.
    Break - vicious - loops.
12. Go VIRTUAL!
    Copy everyone, imitate no-
    one.
    Don't eat the menu!

CHAPTER 15 WHAT DO I NEED TO DO ABOUT MY THINKING?

In which you learn how to think comprehensively

Never knowingly let your change arrive at a place your mind hasn't been before

Obeng

As a Complete Leader you must always think. True you must feel, we discussed that earlier, but you must also think. Thinking is your insurance against mis-leading or not leading. As it says in the quote above, you must never let your change arrive at a place your mind hasn't been before and the way to make this happen is by thinking your way, not just feeling your way.

There are really only five things to think about:

Now let's have a look at each of these elements

1. What I want to say	Write it down here exactly as you would blurt it out

2. What I will actually say …
Purpose (Why is this important / necessary?)
Principles (What are the key things to remember to do / not to do?)
People (Who are the key stakeholders?)
Process (How could it be carried out?)
Performance (What will happen when we have succeeded? How will we know?)

CHAPTER 16   THINKING ABOUT PURPOSE

Leadership is required because there is a "problem."

There are two ways to consider such a problem –

1. as something to be fixed

2. as a doorway to opportunity....

It's Sunday, it's nine o'clock and you're still in bed. A rare treat.   It's been a tough three months. Three tough months in which you have been trying to lead a change initiative which you were 'given' and which if you're honest you're not sure of the merits of. And come to think of it, neither do many other people in the organisation, which has made the going difficult.   But you've soldiered on regardless, especially since you don't know how to push back, stop it or reposition it. On the radio a politician is jousting with the Radio 4 interviewer. 'Amazing', you think, 'don't they ever give it a rest? It's Sunday, the offices are closed and yet they are still announcing 'improvements'.' For a second you feel a pang of jealously. How nice it would be not to have to really deliver but instead to spend your time making presentations and spinning the bad news. Then something in the tone of voice of the interviewer makes you listen to the conversation. In a that single instant you realise

that they could be talking about you and your
change challenge.

Politician:	*'And as a result of poor performance and a number of significant problems caused to the public we have decided to re-organise the department into two areas with a general manager for each'*
Interviewer:	*'But hasn't the poor performance clearly resulted from poor internal communication?' Won't splitting the department exacerbate the problem?'*
Politician:	*'In these cases it is important to act quickly and decisively.' The public insist that something must be done!'*
Interviewer:	*'Yes I agree something must be done but not just anything!' What you're saying is that doing anything is better than doing nothing. It isn't. We need a real solution. There are two ways to solve any problem - you either remove the symptoms or you remove the cause'.*
Politician:	*'But you mustn't lose sight of the opportunity - community leaders and good citizens are expecting to get a faster service as a result of our actions.'*
Interviewer:	*'You say that but the last time you went after improvement opportunities in the health service treatment levers actually fell' I think the man-in-the-street thinks that they will be better off without your improvements'.*

And in that brief moment you realise why you are
having such a tough struggle with your change.

1.   PURPOSE - Fixing a 'problem'

> There are two ways to fix any problem
> You either remove the symptoms
> or you remove the cause
>
> Pentacle

And as a result of poor performance and a number of significant problems caused to the public we have decided to re-organise the department into two areas with a general manager for each.

Mis-Leaders focus on the symptoms, period. They know that they will make an initial splash, gather up some 'low hanging fruit', get some 'brownie points' and then they're off, that's all they care about. They may be aware that fixing symptoms means the problem will re-occur but they may not care about that.

Complete Leaders want to lead real journeys of change, real transformation. This means removing the cause.

There is an old and not very good joke which explains how Complete Leaders approach fixing a problem:

Sherlock Holmes, the great detective and Dr Watson his friend are on a camping holiday. Holmes wakes up in the middle of the night shivering and nudges   Watson awake. "Watson, Watson", he says, "can you see the stars?

"Yes. I can see the stars." replies the sleepy Watson.

"What does that tell you?" demands Holmes.

"It tells me that it is a clear night and that today will be sunny."

"That's not what I meant," splutters Holmes. "I meant what does seeing the stars tell you?"

"It means that the universe is huge out there and we are but a mere speck. Now can I go back to sleep?"

"No and No," says Sherlock, his voice growing impatient. " What does seeing the stars tell you?"

"It means that God has created an enormous firmament?"

"No." says Holmes firmly, "What it tells <u>me</u>," he says shivering, "is that someone has stolen our tent!"

The difference between Holmes and Watson is that Holmes seeks meaning in **causality**, in **why something is happening or has happened** whilst Watson focuses on the **implications** or **effects** of the event.

These two very different approaches are the basis of the method Complete Leaders use to understand a problem prior to resolving it.

The technique is known as BlowingBubbles™.

See if you can read and interpret this diagram:

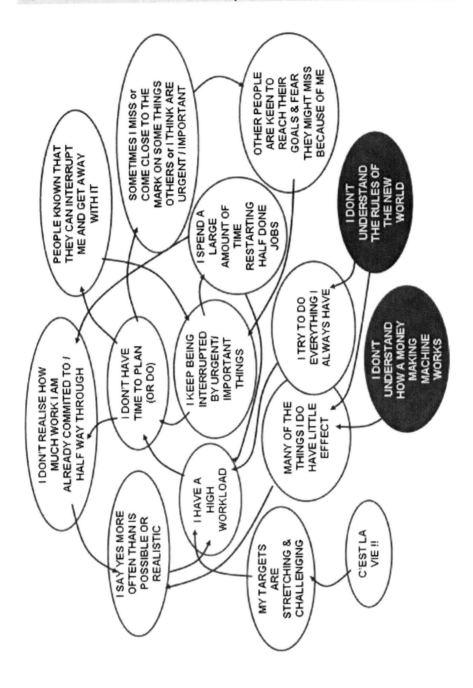

Depressing isn't it? But strange how I know so much about your life, never having met you! The reason is that BubbleDiagrams are fantastic for revealing 'patterns'. Being able to explain 'patterns' and to tell them as 'stories' is a very useful tool for a Complete Leader. **It allows you to eloquently answer the 'why' question.**

Write down, as a sentence, the most obvious symptom (in practice use three symptoms) in a bubble a third of the way from the top of a sheet of A3 paper

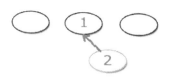

Do a 'Sherlock Holmes' (i.e. ask yourself why this is happening) and write down the cause you found (create bubble 2)

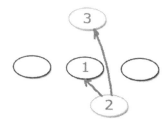

Starting from bubble 2 do a 'Watson' (i.e. if this is the case what else should I expect or if..., <insert the sentence here> then...) This is a new effect (bubble 3). Write it somewhere above bubble 2.

Check that bubble 3 is **TRUE and**

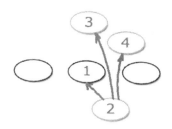

REALLY HAPPENING. If it isn't re-word, rework or delete and redo a 'Holmes' on bubble 2.

Repeat the step above to see what other 'Watsons' (effects) you can come up with (bubble 4) until you have exhausted them all.

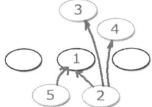

Return to the original symptom (first bubble)

Do a 'Holmes' to try to find another cause (bubble 5)

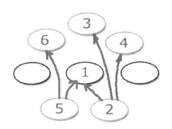

Now do a 'Watson' to confirm the second guess at a cause (bubble 6)

Repeat the sequence 'Holmes' – 'Watson' – 'Watson' until you have run out of ideas for the causes of the first bubble- symptom.

If you have other symptoms move on to those. If not go down one level and work your way across the page horizontally doing Holmes, Watson, Watson, Watson. Then zig-zag downwards.

The more arrows arriving at a bubble (i.e. the more causes to an effect), the more this bubble is to be considered as a true/confirmed fact.

The more arrows leaving a bubble (i.e. the more visible effects to a cause), the more this bubble is to be considered as a true/confirmed fact.

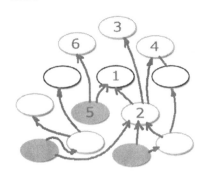

Finally you will arrive at bubbles which are facts of life, historical or arising from a policy, decision, practice or assumption. When you reach these there will be **no arrows pointing at them. This means you have reached the 'anchor' of the problem** (a real root cause). Like all anchors these issues keep the problem alive. Continue until you have unearthed all the anchors (there are rarely more than six).

Focusing on these 'problem-anchors' represents the best way to remove the problem. Dealing with anything else is just mis-leading.

2. PURPOSE - Opening the doorway to Opportunity

Complete Leadership lies in not just solving the problem but seizing the opportunity and delivering more than would have been dreamt of.

There are two common forms and techniques which are useful:

I used to love the 'Wizard of Id' cartoons. One in particular made me laugh. The first frame depicted a messenger arriving at the castle and announcing to the King, "Sire, Sire the peasants are without water." The second another messenger arriving with the message, "Sire, Sire the moat monsters are without food!" The final frame showed the King with a quizzical but evil look on his face thinking "We can work this one out yet!"

Channeling discontent is a way of opening the doorway to opportunity.

Channeling Discontent: Approaches

1. Identify the sources of discontent - physical and emotional

2. Map out the future on your own. If these sources of discontent were removed or reversed (what would happen? what responses would we expect from whom?)

3. Describe why followers feel the discontent

4. Describe what would happen if these were reversed. (How would it look? What would people say? How would people feel?)

5. Make it clear that success is entirely up to them

The second approach is the good old – "I don't just want to stop them beating us up and forcing us to the back of buses" but "I have a dream!" approach Martin Luther King made famous.

Best of all possible worlds: The 'story' structure

The conversation with the followers should follow this structure (copied from Martin Luther King)

1. Current situation

2. Urgency and why it will *not* wait

3. False trails and wrong turns

4. The only choice available is to go forward

5. You must take your own personal needs (describe these) and subsume them in the bigger picture we all face

6. Description of the 'Best of all possible worlds' (How would it look? What would people be saying? How would people feel?)

CHAPTER 17 THINKING ABOUT PRINCIPLES

*A Complete Leader is clear on the limits of acceptability,
what is allowed in the change and what isn't.
A Complete Leader also never undermines the cause by
doing anything which is contrary to the principles of the
cause. Remember: Power corrupts and absolute power
corrupts absolutely – A compromise is a cop-out, a slick
explanation is a sell-out!*

Obeng - Gillet

1.   PRINCIPLES - Setting the limits of acceptability

Followership is dangerous. As a follower:

You put yourself in a position where another person could take advantage of your vulnerabilities - but you're expecting that they will not do this.

You end up making an "exchange" with someone when you do not have full knowledge about them, their intent and the things they are offering to you.

You will be giving something now with an expectation that it will be repaid, possibly in some unspecified way at some unspecified time in the future.

This means the follower must be able to predict what the leader will do in a range of situations. If the follower has a leader they can trust, then they create a safe present and an even better future.

So what this means is that the most effective leaders build trust. But having built this trust, **you must never ever break the trust.** First because this makes you a mis-leader as you bring more misery and broken hearts to the world and ensure that future leaders will have even more difficulty in building trust, and second for your own security. When trust is broken people tend to be pretty vengeful and unforgiving

Trust grows from both a logical and emotional process. In the OldWorld, living and working alongside the same team and colleagues for a couple of decades and knowing other people who could vouch for them or provide insights to their lineage or character meant you could satisfy the logical part of the trust equation. Also interactions over the years would give you a better 'feeling about them'. But sorry, this is the NewWorld - you've just met the people who are supposed to be following you. Or you've not met them but interacted via cyberspace - by phone or email. Or can only reach them in one direction via cyberspace - but television, podcast... How do you build trust and how do you build trust fast?

Before you read this next tool you must swear, hand on heart, never to use it for evil.

Have you done that yet?

Go on then put your hand on your heart...!

To be or not to be trusted. That is the question!

"Do you remember someone you trusted?" "Do you remember why you trusted this person?" When you ask these questions, especially in a business environment, you'll get answers that, for most of them, are converging around the ideas that 'they respected their promises', 'they did what they have said they would do', 'they kept their word'…

Well here it is, the short cut method to building trust fast!

Promise to do
Select an action/ activity which you know for certain you can deliver on within a short (current memory) time-scale. The size of the promise doesn't matter so much: you may think of something reasonably easy and quick to deliver.

Do it
Make sure nothing gets in the way of delivery

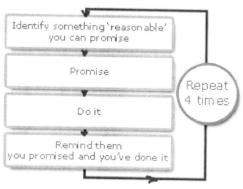

Remind the person that you promised to do it and that you've done it! The two magic words in the added to the title of the email - "As promised"

Repeat three more times with other actions/ activities

Check that trust is built (building)
"Would you feel comfortable with me doing that in your absence?"

Congratulations! You've just built trust! But you will be far more effective if you prepare and plan it in a structured way.

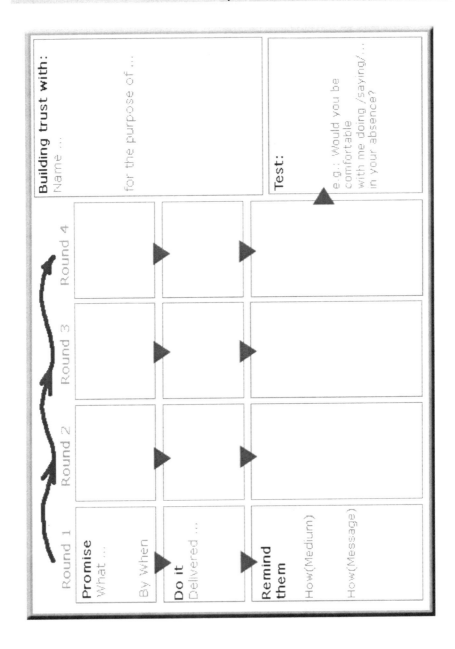

CHAPTER 18 **THINKING** ABOUT **PEOPLE**

> A wise Complete Leader knows 3 truths
> 1.   Not everyone wants to be
> or should be led the same way
> 2.   You can't lead everyone
> 3.   Leadership is very dangerous
> Obeng Gillet

1.   Not everyone should be led the same way

First we need to be really clear on who we have to lead. The easiest route is to **identify the people with a stake either in the current situation or the future situation.** In other words your stakeholders.

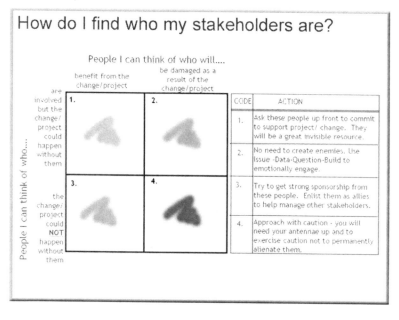

On the right hand panel of the previous image, there is are four one line pieces of advice for dealing with the people you discover in the various boxes of the grid. One piece of advice says **Issue-Data-Question-Build or in short form IDQB**[TM]

This is a technique for **getting turkeys to vote for Christmas**. I invented this technique as a key method for overcoming resistance to change. It is a format for communicating that overcomes resistance and if applied expertly really can actually get turkeys to vote for Christmas!

It pays full respect to the **Third Law of Change**[20] **PEOPLE CREATE CHANGE _ PEOPLE CONSTRAIN CHANGE** described in Chapter 10 on Emotions.

The Third Law of change summarises the impact of change on people - depending on whether it is internally generated or externally imposed.

IDQB[TM] is one of the most effective and popular tools in the Pentacle arsenal. Try it out now. Think of a difficult conversation you have to have with someone. Anything; from a need to improve their performance, to the fact that they will be losing their job.

Use the WorkPad which follows to express your thoughts. Only work in real sentences. No bullet points are allowed. Complete the left hand side first. *[You have consistently failed to follow the processes agreed and have delivered little of value and I'm completely p!$$€&-off!]*

▲ What I will actually say …

Issue
Description of the problem / opportunity

Data
Example to make it clear and un-ambiguous what you're talking about

Question
To trigger engagement

Build
Dialogue

What I want to say …

Write it down here exactly how you would blurt it out

IDQB

Timing:
- all at once
- as far as you can go in one conversation
- one step at a time

Avoiding resistance to change

Then complete the right hand side. Take particular care when completing the **I**ssue to make it as positive, non-surprising and non-threatening as possible (do not sneak in the data/ examples of what is wrong into the issue.) *[I've noticed you've been spending lots of time and energy on the deliverables we agreed last month]*

Now the **D**ata should contain a concrete example(s) of what you've been sidling up to in the Issue. It is a good idea to use an example that the person will instantly recognise. It is also a good idea to use third party examples so it doesn't look like just your opinion. *[However, what you have given me so far is too inaccurate for me to use at all. And Fred tells me that he's told you that when he used what you gave him he lost three clients at a value of £30,000]*

Now for the killer **Q**uestion. What question should you ask to engage the person and allow them to both think about what you have just said and also to speak unaided? A **good** question must not answer itself or be rhetorical (*[Why can't you just apply the processes we've agreed?]* is not good. *[What are you going to do differently as a first step this week to start getting back on track?]* is good)

Have you worked out what you put in the final section? What should you write here?

NOTHING!

You build the dialogue **together**. So nothing can be written here until you actually interact.

Use the grid below to plan the way you will engage your potential followers.

First, take all the stakeholders you've identified using the first stakeholder matrix (at the start of this Chapter) and map them against this second matrix.

Now, you have 4 types of populations for which your approach should significantly differ. Tailor your approaches using the list of hints and tips given in the 'Action' table on the right side of the graphic. You realise now that a large 'kick-off meeting' for everyone is rarely the best way to launch, let's say, a new project...

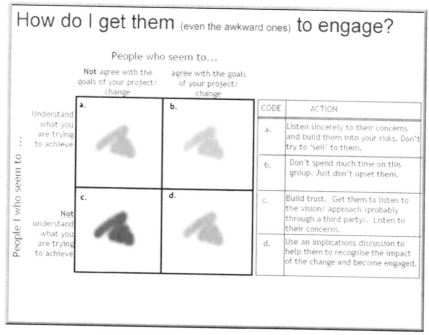

How do I get them (even the awkward ones) to engage?

This time the unfamiliar expression is **Implications Discussion/ ImplicationsQuestions**[TM]

When you've been in discussion with someone, how do you know if your message has been accepted and absorbed? Most people ask questions such as "Are you with me?" "Are you on board?" "Do you understand?" These are pretty pointless questions - the last one especially so. If you tell me something and I understand and you ask, "Do you understand?" I'll say "Yes." but what if I don't understand but have made up my own interpretation which is wrong - I'll still say, "Yes." Or perhaps I'm embarrassed and don't want to say I don't understand I'll still reply, "Yes!" So you walk away thinking you've communicated but in fact you haven't.

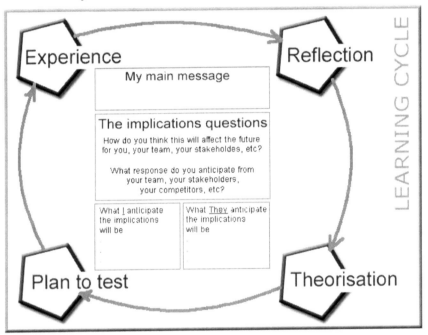

So instead you don't ask about what you've been discussing you ask about their view of the implications of what has been discussed. This is the acid test. They can only answer coherently if they have understood, reflected on what you've said, drawn the principles from it and then thought through how it will affect the future reality. In other words you ask an Implications Question.

An Implications Question forces the recipient round the 4 stage Kolb[21] learning cycle whether they like it or not and gives you a chance to listen to their response and compare it to what you anticipated their response might be.

2. You can't lead everyone

Within the classroom there were certain roles that always had to be filled: the clown, the smelly one no one wanted to sit next to and the king and queen.

If you work out quickly who the king and queen are and you direct all your attention to get them on your side you won't have any discipline problems because everybody follows them.

They don't follow you. They follow them!

Philip Pullman

Most leadership texts suggest that you can lead everyone - in truth you can't. As you will have seen from the grids in the previous section - there are people who don't understand what you are leading to but don't agree anyway. Often their response is emotional and may even have nothing to do with you or the change you're leading but might be a response to a previous change they have experienced or their expectations of what your change might mean to them.

[21] Kolb. D. A. and Fry, R. (1975) 'Toward an applied theory of experiential learning, in C. Cooper (ed.) *Theories of Group Process*, London: John Wiley

This is where ambassadors and third party activists are helpful. As a leader you need to think in terms of dominoes.

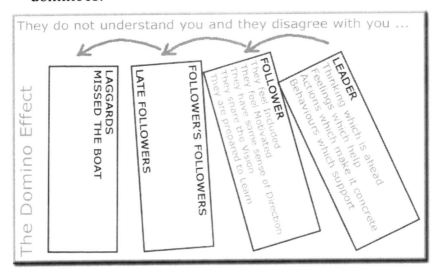

Choose your initial followers carefully - encourage those who have the most appropriate followers themselves. You may need to go out of your way to focus on key individuals who you need to bring others with them.

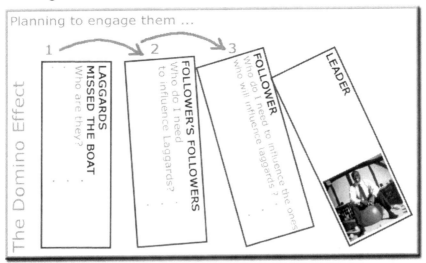

Map out which people or groups of people are in which groups and spend some time making sure that the domino effect will really occur.

3.   Leadership is very dangerous[22]

Life threatening in fact. Think of leaders throughout history. Think how many came to a sticky end. A famous Italian author[23] once wrote a book to advise leaders on how not to end up in a pool of blood.

> 'It should be borne in mind that there is nothing more difficult to arrange, more doubtful of success and more dangerous to carry out than initiating changes in a state's constitution. The innovator makes enemies of all those who prospered under the old order and lukewarm support is forthcoming from those who would prosper under the new.'
> *Nicolo Machiavelli*

He described the level of adulation and support you should expect as you lead complex, world-altering change. This quote hangs on the walls of The Virtual Business School in the UK as a reminder of the difficulty of the task we and the managers we teach are undertaking in transforming the world so that more and more people can understand and enjoy our modern fast-changing, complex NewWorld. We give a copy of it to every person who achieves Master level in our certification programme.

The grid that follows was inspired by his work

---

[22] Benazir Bhutto who was assassinated as we were putting the finishing touches to this Chapter.

[23] *The Prince*. by **Nicolò Machiavelli**. Written c. 1505, published 1515

Nic's Power Grid

	People I have something to give	People I need something from
People more powerful than me	1. Enlist their allegiance in helping to tackle people in box 2 Subtly make sure that they are aware that you are helping them	2. Play your cards close to your chest. Use allegiance. Take your time. Get an honest broker to help present your case.
People less powerful than me	3. You will be able to call on the credits you build here in future	4. Don't waste your advantage by being coercive Use charm or else they will gang up with others against you

CHAPTER 19 THINKING ABOUT PROCESS

> Any journey starts with a single step
> Be sure that step is made by the right person at the right
> time and in the right direction
> *Eddie*
> ... and with the right shoes and the right companions
> *Christophe*

There is a haunting tale we tell of a poor man whom circumstances have chosen to torture. This man is staked down by bungee ropes which are then reinforced  with tough metal chains. Far in the distance he can see the sunlit promised-land he dreams of (perhaps where his love lives? Or, for the French, where the closest 3 star Michelin restaurant is located?) and wishes to reach but unable to break the chains or to cut the bungees. This poor man goes nowhere and simply yearns to be free. However even if he were free, getting to that future would not be so simple for it is a long journey and there is no pre-defined path and the route hides many dangers. Even if he could set off on this dangerous *journey how would he find food and energy and how would he keep going? But for now he's going nowhere for the chains and bungees hold him securely in place. It's sad not reaching your dreams but bearable. And then he feels something climbing up his legs. "It's nothing" he thinks, "just an ant." But before long it becomes an entire column of ants. And not the ordinary kind, these are red soldier ants! "Still it's no cause for alarm", no urgency to move to the better future.*

And then the ants start to bite...

We prefer this analogy of 'ants' to the commonly used term of a 'burning platform'. We've found in real life that there are rarely any real or metaphorical 'burning platforms' just the nuisance of many small things building up. Missed targets, not enough key resource, product launches below par, interest rates rising a fraction when it would be better they fell and so on which lead to the demise of organisations. It is in this indistinct situation that real NewWorld leadership is needed - not when the need to change is obvious to everyone!

The "Red Ant" man as he is known is the centre of the A.N.T.S. checklist for leaders. A.N.T.S. stands for Achieving NewWorld Transformation Success. It is our attempt to capture the overall process a leader must consider to make sure that nothing is left out or left to chance.

It summarises the questions that followers need to have answered.

When we teach it we begin by asking the group what they think the various elements represent and for examples in their own real world. Try it!

ITEM	WHAT DOES IT REPRESENT?	A CONCRETE REAL-LIFE EXAMPLE
The Red Ants		
The Chains		
The Bungee Rope		
Sunlit Distant Land		
The Man		
Uncertain Terrain		
The Unseen Terrain		

What did you discover?

What to Change to?

How to sustain the Change?

Who is to Change?

What to Change (Hard)?

How to make
the Change
happen?
(succesfully)

What to Change (Soft)?

Why Change?

	WHAT HAPPENS IF THIS PART OF THE PROCESS IS MISSING ...?
Why Change?	There is a lack of buy-in and people try to revert to the old ways[24]
What to change (Hard)[25]?	The hard barriers, standard operating procedures, reward mechanism, hierarchical sign-off structures, budget approvals etc. do not get altered and in time the old ways reassert themselves (less common all the hard controls are dropped and anarchy ensues)
What to change (Soft)[26]?	The peer pressure and cultural resistance is never overcome. New heroes do not replace the old and the old myths and legends continue to be told. Eventually the behaviours drift back to the old norms. Occasionally all the culture gets swept aside (see Year Zero or the Chinese cultural revolution) leading to hardship and loss of both knowledge and wisdom. The culture society or group is often irreparably damaged
What to change to?	The change process gets derailed and leads to surprising outcomes (Think USSR where the

---

[24] See discussion on the Third Law of Change (Page 108) and IDQB[TM] on (pages 110 - 112)
[25] See GapLeaping[TM] description on pages 77-82
[26] See Blowing Bubbles[TM] description on pages 95-98

	rallying cry was *What to change* - Perestroika and Glasnost - and not *What to change to* versus Martin Luther King Human Rights Movement[27] where focus was more on what to change to than what to change)
Who[28] has to Change?	Everyone assumes it's someone else when it's them or assumes it's them when it's actually someone else so there is a lot of emotional turmoil and endless speculation and energy sapping gossip
How to make the Change Happen (Successfully)?	There are two elements here: Followers like to know how to contribute and for this reason the leader must have at least the first step People will not follow a leader who looks set for a fall. That is if they are making obvious mistakes or taking easily avoidable risks
How to Sustain the Change?	What happens once you've picked all the low hanging fruit? The change starts with a bang and then fizzles out. The second thing is how do you make or take tough or crossroads decisions? Followers sense the importance of these key decision points and you may lose them if you do not choose wisely

People will not follow a leader who looks set for a fall. That is if they are making obvious mistakes or taking easily avoidable risks

As important as gaining perspective on what needs to happen in the future is the importance of avoiding obvious mistakes. Followers tend not to follow a person or process which has obvious pitfalls. As a leader ignoring these pitfalls and dangers or not responding appropriately can destroy your followership.

---

[27] See the best of all possible worlds
[28] See Stakeholder Identification Grid on Page 107

Did you know that as a Complete Leader you've already been secretly trained to the highest level in risk management and removal?

Science fiction films are a cunning way of training up everyone in the world in risk. Think about it: they all involve aliens. The aliens travel across galaxies to eat you.

Below we have reconstructed scenes from a typical sci-fi movie and then written how we (sensible risk managers) would deal with it and how the people in the films react.

Scene	What we would do...	What happens in Sci-fi films...
Alien space craft crash-lands in a field	We 'Identify this situation as very dangerous' and would either run away or approach it with a lot of caution	They run towards the unfamiliar and obviously dangerous spaceship
We enter and explore the spacecraft and come across a live alien with tentacles, acid, teeth etc.	We would hit it with something hard and 'Kill it immediately' before it gets a chance to eat us.	They take it back to the laboratory for study
We have to find somewhere to stash the alien	We would sealed it in a metal room to 'Contain it'	They leave it on a table in the kitchen
The alien appears to be sleeping	We would brainstorm what to watch out for and	They get the most unsuitable person around to watch it -

	the whole crew would observe the alien closely and continuously. In short we would **Monitor it for any Early Warning signs**	either the pot-smoking 'drongo' who falls asleep or the mad scientist who becomes engrossed in his own measurements of it and doesn't notice it waking up
The alien has escaped from the containment and is now moving around our base killing and eating anyone it comes across	We would move to our **Plan B,** probably to blow up the whole space station	They blow up the whole space station

In summary there are five things we would do to remove risk

Manage risks as you would manage Aliens

1. Identify
2. Fix it (Kill It)! Now!
3. Contain it

4. Monitor it
5. Contingency (Plan B)

CHAPTER 20 **THINKING** ABOUT PERFORMANCE

Tell me how you'll measure and I'll tell you how I'll behave
Tell me when you'll measure me and I'll plan my diary to
make sure I measure up!

The Complete Leader chooses the timings and measurements
carefully to answer the question, "How will I (we) know
when we are succeeding?

There are three ways in which your leadership journey can progress

1 You've started well. Everything goes as envisioned and then you reach a successful outcome. Did this one ever happen to you?

2 You've started well. And everything seems to be going well. You are far too busy and tied up in the journey itself to reflect or review but there's no bad news. You feel great as the journey progresses. Then all of a sudden there's a crisis. Could be anything. But what it means is that for a few days the crisis drives the agenda. For a few worrying days you feel stressed and if you're honest a bit miserable. But you win through and the journey carries on again. You feel great as the journey progresses. Then all of a sudden there's another crisis. Again, could be anything. But what it means is that for a few days the crisis drives the agenda again. For a few worrying days you feel stressed and if you're honest a bit

miserable. But now you're used to a few days of misery every now and then. And now you're back on track you feel great. The journey progresses. Then all of a sudden there's yet another crisis. Again it's triggered by anything. But what it means is that for a few days the crisis drives the agenda. For a few worrying days you feel stressed and if you're honest a bit miserable. But you win through and the journey carries on again...

3 The truth is each crisis arose because you were way off track but without reflecting and reviewing you were blissfully unaware and therefore **you were happy most of the time**.

4 You act like a Complete Leader. Complete Leaders plan-in reflection and review times - and stick to them. The first time you review you discover a minor crisis. You are disappointed if not a little miserable at how things are turning out. Never mind. A bit of work and you're back on the journey. However the next time you check you discover another minor crisis. You are disappointed if not a little miserable at how things are turning out. Never mind. A bit of work and you're back on the journey. In fact, each time you review or reflect

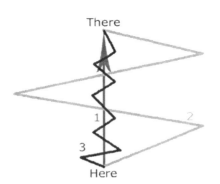

you find bad news! **You are miserable most of the time.**

What you have to understand as a Complete Leader is that if you're not feeling a little disappointed at the current state of affairs on your journey, you're probably making a complete mess of it!

So what exactly should The Complete Leader reflect on?

- Hard (progress toward concrete outcomes)
  Soft (the mood and feelings of the followers)

- Absolute (i.e. "We've created three new businesses.") - Relative (i.e. "It's better than it was.")

- Internal (i.e. people who are participating in the journey) - External (i.e. dispassionate observers not on the journey)

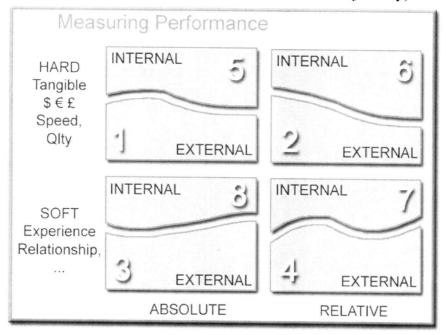

It's a good idea to rely on feedback from more than one direction.

CHAPTER 21   LAST WORDS OF ADVICE TO A COMPLETE LEADER

In which you take time to reflect on success

I must hurry. They have gone and I am their leader

Ghandi

Scientific revolutions (e.g. the earth is not the centre of the universe) were heavily resisted by the community who 'believed' for many reasons, not the least of which is that if you attempt to overturn the established order you will encounter resistance. It is far more fruitful to **add** to the existing beliefs and keep adding until the original belief is patently nonsense. I have done this myself with my revolutionary OldWorld/NewWorld model. Validate the old mind-set of projects with a beginning, a middle and an end. Then add a small dose of reality - "The world is getting faster, how do projects look?" "Now the world is so fast it's faster than we can learn. Now how do projects look?" A big 'aha'. They can't have a beginning a middle and an end - some are very foggy, etc. At this point in the argument people abandon the old orthodoxy and begin to welcome the new. **Always add never subtract. Never offer alternatives.** Later you can de-scope the irrelevant original deliverables

Remember the messenger is the message.

We hope that this is enough.
You are now officially a Complete Leader!

TOPIC
12 RULES FOR THE NEW WORLD
5P's MODEL
ALIEN MODEL
B.E.A.T. MODEL
BEHAVIOURS (The 4 Leadership ...)
BUBBLE DIAGRAM (Problem Solving)
BUSINESS PLAN (Gap Analysis)
CHANGE FRAMEWORK (Red Ant Man)
CHANGE vs IMPROVEMENT
DECISION (Taking the right ...)
DIARY EXERCISE
DOMINO LEADERSHIP
EMOTIONS (Managing my ....)
EUREKA SYNDROME
FOLLOWERS (The 5 triggers for ...)
GAP ANALYSIS
HERE-to-THERE (Reviewing)
IDQB
IMPLICATIONS QUESTIONS
INFLUENCING (IDQB)
ISWON
LEADERS (What they transmit)
LEADERSHIP STYLES (the 4 ...)
LEARNING CYCLE
MINDETS (Managing)
NEW WORLD
OLD WORLD
ONION MAN
ORGANISATION (Context)
PERFORMANCE (Measuring)
PLANNING (Sticky Steps)
POWER GRID
PROBLEM SOLVING (Bubble Diagram)
PROJECT TYPES (The 4 ...)
QUIZ (Leadership Style)
RED ANT MAN
REVIEWING (Here-to-there)
RISK MANAGEMENT (Alien Model)
STAKEHOLDERS (Engagement)
STAKEHOLDERS (Identification)
STICKY STEPS
SURPRISE (Emotions and ....)
TRANSMITTER - RECEIVER MODEL
TRUST (Building ...)

MORE FROM PENTACLE

Pentacle's 5 stage **LearningToTransform**^{TM} approach has gained a stellar reputation for ensuring **real change happens** in organisations. A pragmatic mix of consulting and teaching means that the organisations managers and executives build real skills and knowledge (not just coaching) to apply to their real-life challenges. And the best bit is that unlike a consulting assignment where the consultants take the learning with them once the assignment is over, with LearningToTransform^{TM} you get to keep the learning and use it as much and as long as you wish!

You can find out more about it at:
http://www.pentacle.co.uk/LearningToTransform.htm

And you can read success stories here:
http://www.pentacle.co.uk/Client_Cases.htm

If you wish to explore an original angle to leadership you can register for one of Pentacle's Music and Leadership events.

PentacleTheVBS.com/LeadingFortissimo.htm

And if you wish to prove that you really do make a difference go one step further and become certified by Pentacle.

PentacleTheVBS.com/Certification.htm

Printed in the United Kingdom
by Lightning Source UK Ltd.
126418UK00001B/85-309/P

Karate Kata and Applications 1

By the same authors:
The Karate-do Manual by P. M. V. Morris (Stanley Paul, 1979)
The Advanced Karate Manual (Stanley Paul, 1989)